BK-309

100 Grammar Tickle Stories™

Create Funny Stories with Plurals, Verbs, Is/Are, Was/Were, Comparatives, Superlatives, Possessives, Prepositional Phrases, and Subject/Verb Agreement!

Written by Susan Rose Simms

Edited by Amy Parks and Thomas Webber

Post Office Box 24997, Greenville, SC USA 29616
Call Toll Free 1-800-277-8737 • Fax 1-800-978-7379
 Online! www.superduperinc.com
E-Mail: custserv@superduperinc.com

ISBN# 1-58650-369-3

Introduction

100 Grammar Tickle Stories™

Hilarious! Exciting! Motivating! Imaginative! *Grammar Tickle Stories*™ is all those things and more! This reproducible workbook targets 15 essential grammatical structures in a fun, party game format. Each grammar target has a word list with loads of words for practice and a whimsically illustrated picture word list for non-readers. Each target also includes five unique "tickle" stories and a Companion Activity Sheet that allows students to practice the grammatical forms in their own sentences. Three homework pages accompany each grammar target for extra practice and carry-over. Now get started because time _____!
                                                                                                                (is verb+ing)

How to Use This Book

1. Run off a copy of the word or picture list you're going to use for each student.

2. Run off a copy of the story or stories that you're going to use in the classroom or send home.

3. Run off a copy of the Companion Activity Sheet for the grammar targets you're working on. Students choose words from the word list and write them on the shorter lines. They will use these words in the "tickle" story. After completing the story, students may write their own sentences using these words on the longer lines in the classroom or for homework.

4. Don't reveal the title or the subject of the story ahead of time! That is part of the fun of the surprise.

5. Go around the group and ask each student to supply a grammar target from his or her Companion Activity Sheet.

6. After all the spaces in the story have been filled, reveal the story title.

7. Using the options below, decide how you want to present the story.

Options for Reading Your Funny Story:

1. The SLP or teacher reads the story aloud. Students will recognize their contributions to the story!

2. The SLP or teacher reads the story aloud, pausing at the fill-in spaces. Students say the grammar targets aloud as a group or while taking turns.

3. Students take turns reading the story, line by line. Either run off a copy for everyone or pass it on down!

4. Create your own special ways to share the story. Your students will have their own favorites!

#BK-309 Grammar Tickle Stories™ • ©2004 Super Duper® Publications • 1-800-277-8737 • Online! www.superduperinc.com

Expansion Suggestions

Even though the stories were written with a certain grammatical form in mind, other forms might pop up while talking about the stories.

1. After reading a story, ask your students "Which word(s) would make more sense here?" For example, in "Present-ing New Nursery Rhymes," a student may choose "is combing" for the first blank. The sentence will read "Little Boy Blue is combing his horn." Ask "Which word would make more sense here?" Your student might say "is blowing" or "is carrying."

2. There are five questions in each story and about five fill-in spaces. Many stories have more than five spaces. Ask more questions to include all fill-in spaces. This will give students extra practice using their grammar targets.

3. Have your students draw a picture of their funny story or their favorite "tickle" sentence.

4. After reading a story, ask your students "Why is that silly?"

Homework Activity Cards

Each section has two pages of four homework activity cards (8 total). Make a copy of a page with your student's grammar target and cut out the cards. Send as many cards home with the student as desired. Have students bring completed activity cards back to school. Here are suggestions for more activity card fun:

1. Punch a hole in each one and insert a ring. Review the cards regularly to practice skills.

2. Staple the activity cards together on the left side to make a small booklet. Have your student design an original cover. Read the booklet regularly for extra practice.

Combo Sections

The following grammar targets have combo sections: Regular and Irregular Plurals, Is and Are Verb+ing, Was and Were Verb+ing, Regular and Irregular Past Tense Verbs, Subject/Verb Agreement Singular, and Subject/Verb Agreement Plural. Use the word lists (or picture word lists for non-readers) from both sections when choosing words for the combo section. For example: Use the word lists from Regular Plurals and Irregular Plurals while working on the Plural Combo section.

The Comparatives and Superlatives section (pages 57-78) has one picture word list and one word list (pages 59-60). The page is divided into the base word, -er, and -est columns. Use the base and -er columns in the Comparatives activities. Use all three columns (base, -er, and -est) in the Superlatives section.

Table of Contents

#BK-309 Grammar Tickle Stories™ • ©2004 Super Duper® Publications • 1-800-277-8737 • Online! www.superduperinc.com

Parent/Helper Letter

Dear Parent/Helper,

    Here is a homework assignment that both you and your child are going to love! Your child has brought home a *Grammar Tickle Story*™. This is a fun way for your child to practice his/her grammar targets. First, ask your child to pick words from his/her word or picture list to fill in the blanks in the story. (Don't show the story to your child. Have them write the words on the Companion Activity Sheet, or you write them into the story blanks.) Then, read the story together with the words in place. The result is a story sure to tickle your funny bone!

Please complete the item(s) checked below:

- ❏ Complete this story at home with your child as indicated above. Ask your child to supply words from the word or picture list.

- ❏ Also, have your child fill out the Companion Activity Sheet. You may write your child's response for him/her if needed.

- ❏ Go over the questions at the end of the story. Be sure your child answers in a complete sentence.

- ❏ Have your child complete the Companion Activity Sheet by writing (or saying for non-writers) a sentence on each of the lines provided.

When you are finished with the story, or if your child brings home a completed story, do the following:

- ❏ Read the story to your child.

- ❏ Have your child read the story.

- ❏ Read the story to your child and pause at each fill-in-the-blank space. Allow your child to fill in the blank aloud with a new word from the word or picture list.

- ❏ Have your child fill-in-the-blank with the words written on the Companion Activity Sheet each time you pause.

Thanks for your help at home! Have fun!

Regular and Irregular Plurals

Regular Plurals

Directions: Use the picture words below to help you complete the stories on pages 4 to 8 and 24 to 28.

airplane**s**

books

cookie**s**

horse**s**

apple**s**

brush**es**

cow**s**

house**s**

ball**s**

bus**es**

cup**s**

rabbit**s**

banana**s**

car**s**

dog**s**

spoon**s**

bed**s**

cat**s**

doll**s**

tree**s**

bird**s**

chair**s**

pencil**s**

truck**s**

Regular
Plurals

#BK-309 Grammar Tickle Stories™ • ©2004 Super Duper® Publications • 1-800-277-8737 • Online! www.superduperinc.com

Regular Plurals

Directions: Use these words to help complete the stories on pages 4 to 8 and pages 24 to 28.

❏ airplanes
❏ angels
❏ apples
❏ arms
❏ balloons
❏ balls
❏ bananas
❏ baseballs
❏ beds
❏ bells
❏ bikes
❏ birds
❏ blocks
❏ boats
❏ boots
❏ boys
❏ bushes
❏ cakes
❏ carrots
❏ cars
❏ cats
❏ chairs
❏ chickens
❏ clocks
❏ clowns
❏ coats
❏ combs
❏ computers
❏ cookies
❏ cows

❏ crayons
❏ cups
❏ desks
❏ dogs
❏ dolls
❏ doors
❏ doughnuts
❏ drums
❏ ducks
❏ ears
❏ eggs
❏ eyes
❏ flags
❏ flowers
❏ forks
❏ girls
❏ goats
❏ hammers
❏ hands
❏ hats
❏ horses
❏ houses
❏ keys
❏ lions
❏ monkeys
❏ nails
❏ napkins
❏ oranges
❏ pencils
❏ pens

❏ pickles
❏ pictures
❏ pigs
❏ pillows
❏ plants
❏ plates
❏ puzzles
❏ rabbits
❏ rocks
❏ roses
❏ rugs
❏ shirts
❏ shoes
❏ skates
❏ slides
❏ snakes
❏ snowballs
❏ socks
❏ spiders
❏ spoons
❏ swings
❏ tables
❏ tails
❏ teachers
❏ towels
❏ trains
❏ wagons
❏ wheels
❏ whistles
❏ worms

Regular Plurals

The Annual Family Picnic Newsletter

Directions: Give each student a list of the Picture Words on page 2 or the Word List on page 3. Do not reveal the story title. Ask each student for "words" from his/her page to fill in the spaces in the story below. Write the words in the spaces. You may also have the student write these words on his/her Companion Activity Sheet (page 9). Then, have the student read/listen to the story. For more options, see *How To Use This Book* on page ii.

Dear Family Members,

We hope to see you at the Annual Family Picnic. Here are highlights from last year

at Grover's Park. Uncle Max brought some _____ to feed the ducks.

(regular plural)

Cousins Sally and Bo brought the _____ they won from their soccer

(regular plural)

season. We tossed _____ and, as usual, Grandpa Stewart and little

(regular plural)

Stevie, Jr. were the only ones who didn't drop any! We even had _____ for

(regular plural)

the dogs to fetch! We had our White Elephant Gift Give Away! Poppy Al gave his

_____ away to Aunt Lil, who picked the winning ticket. Aunt Lil, who had

(regular plural)

wrapped up her _____ in newspaper, gave them to a surprised Grandma

(regular plural)

Nons! Next year, we will have the flying contest with_____. So get your

(regular plural)

_____ out of mothballs and start practicing. You also might want to bring

(regular plural)

your own picnic lunch this year. Uncle Burnsit is in charge of the barbecue!

Love,

Grandma Dilly

Questions: (Answer in a complete sentence.)

❑ 1. What did Uncle Max bring last year to feed the ducks?

❑ 2. What did the dogs have to fetch?

❑ 3. What did Poppy Al give to Aunt Lil?

❑ 4. What will you fly in the flying contest?

❑ 5. What should you get "out of mothballs" to start practicing?

Homework: Take a copy of this story and word/picture list home, and follow the directions above.

Name	Homework Partner	Date

Regular Plurals

#BK-309 Grammar Tickle Stories™ • ©2004 Super Duper® Publications • 1-800-277-8737 • Online! www.superduperinc.com

Throwing Snowballs

Directions: Give each student a list of the Picture Words on page 2 or the Word List on page 3. Do not reveal the story title. Ask each student for "words" from his/her page to fill in the spaces in the story below. Write the words in the spaces. You may also have the student write these words on his/her Companion Activity Sheet (page 9). Then, have the student read/listen to the story. For more options, see *How To Use This Book* on page ii.

I love the snow. Best of all, I love throwing snowballs. I like to make snowballs look

like _____. My brother and I take huge balls of snow and pile them up to
      (regular plural)

look like _____. My parents laugh and say, "I love your _____!"
      (regular plural)   (regular plural)

They are silly. My brother and I lie down in the snow and make snow _____,
                                             (regular plural)

moving our arms and legs around. Later, we go inside and have hot cocoa. As the

whipped cream melts, it looks like _____ swimming around! Sometimes the
                      (regular plural)

snow piles up on the _____ and Dad has to go outside and shovel them.
           (regular plural)

My brother and I put our noses to the window and breathe on it. Then, we draw

_____ on the glass! Sometimes icicles hang down from the roof and look
(regular plural)

like rows of _____! And that's "snow kidding!"
      (regular plural)

Questions: (Answer in a complete sentence.)

❏ 1. What does the sister like to make snowballs look like?

❏ 2. What do the brother and sister make out of large snowballs?

❏ 3. What do the brother and sister make by lying down in the snow and moving their arms and legs?

❏ 4. What do the melting, whipped cream shapes look like?

❏ 5. What do the brother and sister draw with their breath on the window?

Homework: Take a copy of this story and word/picture list home, and follow the directions above.

_____   _____   _____   **Regular Plurals**
Name   Homework Partner   Date

As Easy As Riding a Bike

Directions: Give each student a list of the Picture Words on page 2 or the Word List on page 3. Do not reveal the story title. Ask each student for "words" from his/her page to fill in the spaces in the story below. Write the words in the spaces. You may also have the student write these words on his/her Companion Activity Sheet (page 9). Then, have the student read/listen to the story. For more options, see *How To Use This Book* on page ii.

So, you've decided that today's the day to take off those training wheels and set out on

your own two wheeler! Here are some pointers to help you. First, be sure you wear a

good set of protective _____ on your elbows and padded _____
                                                   (regular plural)   (regular plural)

on your knees. Take your bike on the sidewalk and steady the _____ as you
                                                            (regular plural)

gently swing your leg over the seat. Make sure the _____ are facing in the
                                                    (regular plural)

direction you want to go. To help you steer nice and straight, grip the _____
                                                                (regular plural)

and hold them steady. In one swift motion, put your feet on the _____ and
                                                          (regular plural)

start pedaling them as you gently lower into the seat. At first you might feel a little rocky,

but keep your eye on the _____ ahead. Soon you'll feel the breeze through
                                        (regular plural)

your _____ and yell, "Look Mom and Dad, I'm riding a bike!"
                 (regular plural)

Questions: (Answer in a complete sentence.)
- ❏ 1. What should you wear on your elbows?
- ❏ 2. What should you wear on your knees?
- ❏ 3. What should be facing in the direction you want to go?
- ❏ 4. What should you put your feet on and start pedaling?
- ❏ 5. What will you feel the breeze run through?

Homework: Take a copy of this story and word/picture list home, and follow the directions above.

<table>
<tr><td>_____</td><td>_____</td><td>_____</td><td rowspan="2">**Regular Plurals**</td></tr>
<tr><td>Name</td><td>Homework Partner</td><td>Date</td></tr>
</table>

#BK-309 Grammar Tickle Stories™ • ©2004 Super Duper® Publications • 1-800-277-8737 • Online! www.superduperinc.com

Clowning Around

Directions: Give each student a list of the Picture Words on page 2 or the Word List on page 3. Do not reveal the story title. Ask each student for "words" from his/her page to fill in the spaces in the story below. Write the words in the spaces. You may also have the student write these words on his/her Companion Activity Sheet (page 9). Then, have the student read/listen to the story. For more options, see *How To Use This Book* on page ii.

Welcome to *Clown School!* In front of you is a box with all the necessary things a

good clown needs. First, all clowns wear _____ on their nose. Please
(regular plural)

take those out and stick them right on the end of your nose. Next, you'll see different

colored _____. Those go on your head. You're starting to look like a clown
(regular plural)

already! Take out the colored wax and draw some _____ on your cheeks!
(regular plural)

I'm starting to laugh even now! Since you can't talk, you need things to make noise. So,

take out the _____ and the _____ and squeeze them. Isn't
(regular plural)   (regular plural)

that a funny sound? And what clown would be complete without a big set of

_____ on his or her feet? Clowns do funny things like squirting pretend
(regular plural)

_____ and squeezing into _____. Now, who volunteered to
(regular plural)   (regular plural)

be shot out of a cannon?

Questions: (Answer in a complete sentence.)

❑ 1. What did the clowns put on their noses?
❑ 2. What different colored things did the clowns put on their heads?
❑ 3. What did the clowns draw on their cheeks?
❑ 4. What did the clowns squeeze that made noise?
❑ 5. What did the clowns put on their feet?

Homework: Take a copy of this story and word/picture list home, and follow the directions above.

_____   _____   _____   **Regular Plurals**
Name   Homework Partner   Date

Old King Cole Loses His Cool

Directions: Give each student a list of the Picture Words on page 2 or the Word List on page 3. Do not reveal the story title. Ask each student for "words" from his/her page to fill in the spaces in the story below. Write the words in the spaces. You may also have the student write these words on his/her Companion Activity Sheet (page 9). Then, have the student read/listen to the story. For more options, see *How To Use This Book* on page ii.

Old King Cole was a merry old soul...but on one particular day, Cole lost his cool.

King Cole called for his _____. Then, he called for his _____
                           (regular plural)   (regular plural)

and three of his _____. All the fiddlers were suddenly missing. They had
                   (regular plural)

very fine _____. Along came the Queen of _____ with a
            (regular plural)   (regular plural)

similar problem. Her trusty Knave of Hearts had run off with her _____.
                                                       (regular plural)

They put out a bulletin to find the fiddlers and the Knave of Hearts, offering one hundred

_____. Later, the fiddlers and the Knave of Hearts came back bringing
(regular plural)

each other for the the reward! "This is puzzling," said a very upset King Cole. "Let's stay

cool, Cole," said the Queen. "I know what we'll do." She brought out some

_____. "Now there's enough for everyone!" The fiddlers started playing
(regular plural)

and the celebration began. King Cole was a merry old soul once again.

Questions: (Answer in a complete sentence.)

❏ 1. What did King Cole call for first?

❏ 2. What did King Cole's fiddlers have?

❏ 3. What did the Knave of Hearts run off with?

❏ 4. What reward was offered?

❏ 5. What did the Queen bring out as a second reward?

Homework: Take a copy of this story and word/picture list home, and follow the directions above.

_____ _____ _____

Name   Homework Partner   Date

Regular Plurals

#BK-309 Grammar Tickle Stories™ • ©2004 Super Duper® Publications • 1-800-277-8737 • Online! www.superduperinc.com

Regular Plurals Companion Activity Sheet

Directions: During or following the story, have the student write words from the word or picture list on the lines below. Then, have the student write sentences with these words in them.

Example: _____ ***cookies*** _____

*I ate all of the peanut butter **cookies** out of the cookie jar.*

1. _____

_____

2. _____

_____

3. _____

_____

4. _____

_____

5. _____

_____

6. _____

_____

7. _____

_____

8. _____

_____

Homework: Take a copy of this sheet home with a word/picture list. Then, follow the directions above.

_____ _____ _____

Name   Homework Partner   Date

Regular Plurals

Perfectly Paired

Directions: Look at the pictures on the left and say the word. Then, match the single form of the word to the picture on the right that shows more than one. Write the word in its plural form. Then, draw a line to connect them, or color each matching pair with a different color!

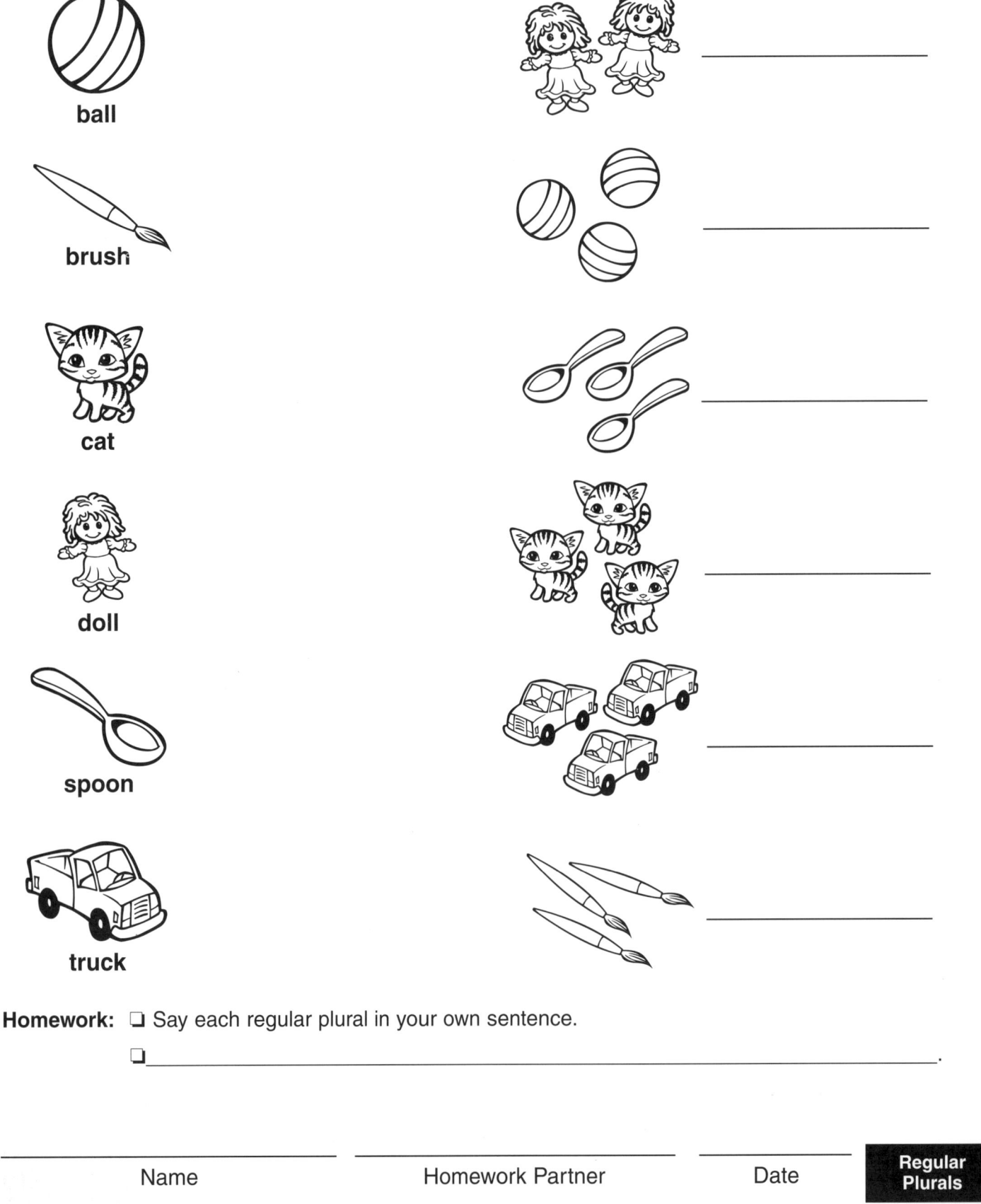

ball

brush

cat

doll

spoon

truck

Homework: ❑ Say each regular plural in your own sentence.

❑ _____.

_____   _____   _____
Name   Homework Partner   Date

Regular Plurals

#BK-309 Grammar Tickle Stories™ • ©2004 Super Duper® Publications • 1-800-277-8737 • Online! www.superduperinc.com

Regular Plurals

Fill in the blanks in the sentences with the regular plural form of the underlined nouns (<u>cat</u>, <u>cat**s**</u>). Then, read the complete sentences.

I have a <u>doll</u> and my sister has a <u>doll</u>. We have two _____. We like to dress our two _____ in matching outfits!

(Bonus Activity: Talk about your toys.)

_____
Name

_____
Date

Regular Plurals

Fill in the blanks in the sentences with the regular plural form of the underlined nouns (<u>cat</u>, <u>cat**s**</u>). Then, read the complete sentences.

My mom drives a <u>car</u> and my dad drives a <u>car</u>. They have two _____. They drive their _____ to work.

(Bonus Activity: Talk about cars.)

_____
Name

_____
Date

Regular Plurals

Fill in the blanks in the sentences with the regular plural form of the underlined nouns (<u>cat</u>, <u>cat**s**</u>). Then, read the complete sentences.

I found a <u>shell</u> on the beach yesterday and I found another <u>shell</u> today. Now I have two _____. If I put the two _____ up to my ears, I can hear the ocean!

(Bonus Activity: Talk about things you can make with shells.)

_____
Name

_____
Date

Regular Plurals

Fill in the blanks in the sentences with the regular plural form of the underlined nouns (<u>cat</u>, <u>cat**s**</u>). Then, read the complete sentences.

I threw a <u>snowball</u> and my brother threw a <u>snowball</u>. Then the two _____ hit each other! We took our two _____ and started building a snowman!

(Bonus Activity: Talk about something else fun to do with snowballs.)

_____
Name

_____
Date

Regular Plurals

Regular Plurals

Fill in the blanks in the sentences with the regular plural form of the underlined nouns (c<u>at</u>, c<u>ats</u>). Then, read the complete sentences.

My best friend has a blue <u>bike</u> and my neighbor has a red <u>bike</u>. I like both of their _____! We all ride our _____ on the sidewalk.

(*Bonus Activity: Why is it safer to ride bikes on the sidewalk?*)

_____
Name

_____
Date

Regular Plurals

Fill in the blanks in the sentences with the regular plural form of the underlined nouns (c<u>at</u>, c<u>ats</u>). Then, read the complete sentences.

The clown threw one <u>ball</u> in the air. Then, he threw another <u>ball</u> and another <u>ball</u>. Soon he was juggling all three _____ in the air! He didn't drop any of the _____!

(*Bonus Activity: Talk about some other things you can do with balls.*)

_____
Name

_____
Date

Regular Plurals

Fill in the blanks in the sentences with the regular plural form of the underlined nouns (c<u>at</u>, c<u>ats</u>). Then, read the complete sentences.

I saw an <u>ant</u> carry off a scrap of food at our family picnic. Another <u>ant</u> was right behind him. Soon there were a whole colony of _____! We didn't let all those _____ ruin our picnic!

(*Bonus Activity: Why do you think ants like picnics?*)

_____
Name

_____
Date

Regular Plurals

Fill in the blanks in the sentences with the regular plural form of the underlined nouns (c<u>at</u>, c<u>ats</u>). Then, read the complete sentences.

Old King Cole called for one <u>fiddler</u>, then he called for another <u>fiddler</u>. He listened to both of his _____ play a happy song. Those _____ played so that Old King Cole could dance.

(*Bonus Activity: What are some other instruments you know about?*)

_____
Name

_____
Date

Regular Plurals

Irregular Plurals

Directions: Use the picture words below to help you complete the stories on pages 15 to 19 and pages 24 to 28.

calves	firemen	leaves	policemen
children	fish	loaves	sheep
deer	geese	men	shelves
elves	hooves	mice	teeth
feet	knives	moose	women

Irregular
Plurals

Irregular Plurals

Directions: Use these words to help complete the stories on pages 15 to 19 and pages 24 to 28.

- buffalo
- calves
- children
- deer
- dice
- elves
- feet
- firemen
- fish
- geese
- halves
- hooves
- knives
- leaves
- lives
- loaves
- men
- mice
- moose
- oxen
- people
- policemen
- reindeer
- salmon
- scarves
- selves
- sheep
- shelves
- shrimp
- teeth
- thieves
- wives
- wolves
- women

Irregular
Plurals

#BK-309 Grammar Tickle Stories™ • ©2004 Super Duper® Publications • 1-800-277-8737 • Online! www.superduperinc.com

The Sunday Sale

Directions: Give each student a list of the Picture Words on page 13 or the Word List on page 14. Do not reveal the story title. Ask each student for "words" from his/her page to fill in the spaces in the story below. Write the words in the spaces. You may also have the student write these words on his/her Companian Activity Sheet (page 20). Then, have the student read/listen to the story. For more options, see *How To Use This Book* on page ii.

SUNDAY SALE NOTICE

We'd like everyone to sign up for our annual neighborhood Sunday sale.   Last year

Mrs. Wigglesby sold all of her _____! She used her money to buy
(irregular plural)

_____ for her entire family.   Mr. Barnsworth hauled out the
(irregular plural)

_____ from his garage. His neighbor, Miss Sippleton, liked them so
(irregular plural)

much, she traded all her _____ for them! So far, the following
(irregular plural)

people have signed up:

1. Henry Hatsoff is selling his collection of 16 _____.
(irregular plural)

2. Jenny Whatzwithit wants to sell her set of _____.
(irregular plural)

3. Old Mr. Coopedup is going to get rid of all the _____

cluttering up his backyard!
(irregular plural)

4. _____ has one dozen _____
(your name)   (irregular plural)

for sale!

Questions: (Answer in a complete sentence.)
- ❏ 1. What did Mrs. Wigglesby sell last year?
- ❏ 2. What did Mr. Barnsworth and Mrs. Sippleton trade?
- ❏ 3. What is Henry Hatsoff selling?
- ❏ 4. What is Mr. Coopedup finally going to get rid of?
- ❏ 5. What are YOU going to sell?

Homework: Take a copy of this story and word/picture list home, and follow the directions above.

_____   _____   _____
Name   Homework Partner   Date

Irregular Plurals

Things Went Swimmingly!

Directions: Give each student a list of the Picture Words on page 13 or the Word List on page 14. Do not reveal the story title. Ask each student for "words" from his/her page to fill in the spaces in the story below. Write the words in the spaces. You may also have the student write these words on his/her Companion Activity Sheet (page 20). Then, have the student read/listen to the story. For more options, see *How To Use This Book* on page ii.

Yesterday our class went to the aquarium. We packed up our _____

(irregular plural)

and got on the bus. When we got there, the guide told us to leave the _____

(irregular plural)

on the bus because we wouldn't need them. The first place we went was the

_____ Tank. It was fun to watch them swim and dive for food. At the

(irregular plural)

Touching Tank, we were allowed to feel the _____. Our teacher said they

(irregular plural)

felt like the _____ we read about in our science books! We got to see the

(irregular plural)

_____, who come only once a year to feed. At the end of our tour, we went

(irregular plural)

to the Gift Shop. There were so many stuffed _____ to choose from, I

(irregular plural)

couldn't decide. So I ended up buying a book about _____ because I

(irregular plural)

thought they were the most interesting things I saw on our tour.

Questions: (Answer in a complete sentence.)
- ❏ 1. What did we pack up before we got on the bus?
- ❏ 2. What is the first place we went at the aquarium?
- ❏ 3. What did we get to touch at the Touching Tank?
- ❏ 4. What kind of stuffed animals were on sale at the gift shop?
- ❏ 5. What book did the writer end up buying and why?

Homework: Take a copy of this story and word/picture list home, and follow the directions above.

Name	Homework Partner	Date

Irregular Plurals

#BK-309 Grammar Tickle Stories™ • ©2004 Super Duper® Publications • 1-800-277-8737 • Online! www.superduperinc.com

Art Class

Directions: Give each student a list of the Picture Words on page 13 or the Word List on page 14. Do not reveal the story title. Ask each student for "words" from his/her page to fill in the spaces in the story below. Write the words in the spaces. You may also have the student write these words on his/her Companion Activity Sheet (page 20). Then, have the student read/listen to the story. For more options, see *How To Use This Book* on page ii.

Today we're going to learn how to make clay _____. It's easier than you
(irregular plural)

think! Remember last week when we made the paper plate _____? You
(irregular plural)

thought THAT would be difficult before you actually did it! Now, if you mold the clay when

it's too hard, your artwork could turn out to look more like _____ . So first,
(irregular plural)

turn to page 25 in your books and look at the picture of the _____. A
(irregular plural)

famous artist studied the habits of the _____ for years before attempting to
(irregular plural)

make this. We'll do it by closing our eyes and picturing many _____ playing
(irregular plural)

in the park. Now, take your markers and paper and draw some _____. You
(irregular plural)

are now ready to transfer this to clay. Next week we're going to learn to make

_____ statues out of wire clothes hangers!
(irregular plural)

Questions: (Answer in a complete sentence.)

❏ 1. What is the class going to learn to make today?

❏ 2. What did the class make out of paper plates last week?

❏ 3. What was in the picture on page 25?

❏ 4. What did you picture playing in the park?

❏ 5. What are you going to make out of wire clothes hangers next week?

Homework: Take a copy of this story and word/picture list home, and follow the directions above.

_____   _____   _____ | Irregular Plurals |

Name   Homework Partner   Date

Surprise Party Invitation

Directions: Give each student a list of the Picture Words on page 13 or the Word Lists on page 14. Do not reveal the story title. Ask each student for "words" from his/her page to fill in the spaces in the story below. Write the words in the spaces. You may also have the student write these words on his/her Companion Activity Sheet (page 20). Then, have the student read/listen to the story. For more options, see *How To Use This Book* on page ii.

I am having a surprise party for _____. We'll play *Pin The Ears On The*
(Name)

_____. Then, we will have a big scavenger hunt to look for things like
(irregular plural)

_____ and _____. _____ will hit a piñata and
(irregular plural)   (irregular plural)   (Name)

chocolate _____ will fall out! Here are some gift ideas. _____
(irregular plural)   (Name)

collects miniature _____. She also likes stuffed _____. For
(irregular plural)   (irregular plural)

dessert, we'll have a special cake! It will be decorated with colorful _____.
(irregular plural)

We will end the party with *Ring Around The* _____ and everyone will sing
(irregular plural)

"Happy Birthday." But remember, it's a surprise! Don't tell _____!
(Name)

Questions: (Answer in a complete sentence.)

❏ 1. What will you "pin the ears on" during the game?

❏ 2. What will you look for on your scavenger hunt?

❏ 3. What will come out of the piñata?

❏ 4. What does the birthday person like?

❏ 5. What is the last game that will be played at the party?

Homework: Take a copy of this story and word/picture list home, and follow the directions above.

_____   _____   _____   **Irregular**
Name   Homework Partner   Date   **Plurals**

At The Pet Store

Directions: Give each student a list of the Picture Words on page 13 or the Word Lists on page 14. Do not reveal the story title. Ask each student for "words" from his/her page to fill in the spaces in the story below. Write the words in the spaces. You may also have the student write these words on his/her Companion Activity Sheet (page 20). Then, have the student read/listen to the story. For more options, see *How To Use This Book* on page ii.

I love going to the Pet Shop! I always see a lot of colorful _____ for my
(irregular plural)

dog. She loves to chase them. She also buries them next to her _____ and
(irregular plural)

then we can't find them. My brother Jamie likes to buy new _____ for his
(irregular plural)

fish tank. The fish love to swim around them! My sister Chloe buys _____
(irregular plural)

to put in her hamster cage and the hamsters run around them! One time she had a

whole bunch of _____ that got out and were all over the house. It was a
(irregular plural)

mess! My mom screamed because she thought they were _____! Today,
(irregular plural)

the Pet Shop was having a special on _____ and my dad couldn't resist.
(irregular plural)

He thought they would go great in the bird cage with the _____. Yep, the
(irregular plural)

trip to the Pet Shop is always an adventure!

Questions: (Answer in a complete sentence.)

❏ 1. What colorful things did the writer see for his dog?

❏ 2. What did Jamie buy for his fish tank?

❏ 3. What did Chloe buy for her hamster?

❏ 4. What was on special at the pet store?

❏ 5. What was in the bird cage?

Homework: Take a copy of this story and word/picture list home, and follow the directions above.

_____ _____ _____

Name   Homework Partner   Date

| Irregular Plurals |

Irregular Plurals Companion Activity Sheet

Directions: During or following the story, have the student write words from the word or picture list on the lines below. Then, have the student write sentences with these words in them.

Example: _____ *mice* _____

*The mouse shared the cheese with three hungry **mice**.*

1. _____

_____

2. _____

_____

3. _____

_____

4. _____

_____

5. _____

_____

6. _____

_____

7. _____

_____

8. _____

_____

Homework: Take a copy of this sheet home with a word/picture list. Then, follow the directions above.

_____ _____ _____

| Name | Homework Partner | Date |

Irregular Plurals

#BK-309 Grammar Tickle Stories™ • ©2004 Super Duper® Publications • 1-800-277-8737 • Online! www.superduperinc.com

Counting Sheep

Directions: Today, Shauna learned about irregular plurals. She is even dreaming about them, but she can't remember all of them. Please help her get a good night's sleep by circling the correct irregular plural on each sheep.

Homework: ❏ Say each irregular plural in your own sentence.

❏ _____.

_____   _____   _____

Name   Homework Partner   Date

Irregular Plurals

Fill in the blanks in the sentences with the irregular plural form of the underlined nouns (calf, calves). Then, read the complete sentences.

The policeman needed backup, so he called _____ to join him. All the other _____ came to help the policeman.

(Bonus Activity: Why do we need policemen?)

_____ _____
Name   Date

Irregular Plurals

Fill in the blanks in the sentences with the irregular plural form of the underlined nouns (calf, calves). Then, read the complete sentences.

One little fish swam up to get the food, and all the other _____ followed him. Many _____ were eating the food.

(Bonus Activity: Where are some places you can see fish?)

_____ _____
Name   Date

Irregular Plurals

Fill in the blanks in the sentences with the irregular plural form of the underlined nouns (calf, calves). Then, read the complete sentences.

I set the table with one knife, but we needed four _____. There were four _____ at our table.

(Bonus Activity: Tell your homework partner how many knives are on the table.)

_____ _____
Name   Date

Irregular Plurals

Fill in the blanks in the sentences with the irregular plural form of the underlined nouns (calf, calves). Then, read the complete sentences.

After one leaf fell to the ground, all the other _____ started falling. We raked all the _____ into a pile, after they fell to the ground.

(Bonus Activity: Why is it fun to jump in a pile of leaves?)

_____ _____
Name   Date

Irregular Plurals

#BK-309 Grammar Tickle Stories™ • ©2004 Super Duper® Publications • 1-800-277-8737 • Online! www.superduperinc.com

Irregular Plurals

Fill in the blanks in the sentences with the irregular plural form of the underlined nouns (calf, calves). Then, read the complete sentences.

I have a left foot and a right foot, so I have

two _____. I have new shoes to wear on my

two _____.

(Bonus Activity: What are some things you can do with your feet?)

_____ _____
Name   Date

Irregular Plurals

Fill in the blanks in the sentences with the irregular plural form of the underlined nouns (calf, calves). Then, read the complete sentences.

I lost one tooth, but my brother lost two

_____ because he's older. My brother put

both of his _____ under his pillow, after they

fell out.

(Bonus Activity: How do you take care of your teeth?)

_____ _____
Name   Date

Irregular Plurals

Fill in the blanks in the sentences with the irregular plural form of the underlined nouns (calf, calves). Then, read the complete sentences.

The wolf lives in the forest with the other

_____. There are many _____ that live

in the forest.

(Bonus Activity: What do wolves look like?)

_____ _____
Name   Date

Irregular Plurals

Fill in the blanks in the sentences with the irregular plural form of the underlined nouns (calf, calves). Then, read the complete sentences.

There was a new child in our class, so now we

have 32 _____ in our class. Thirty two is a lot

of _____ in one class!

(Bonus Activity: How many children are in your class?)

_____ _____
Name   Date

Irregular Plurals

Step Right Up!

Directions: Give each student a list of the Picture Words on pages 2 and 13 or the Word Lists on pages 3 and 14. Do not reveal the story title. Ask each student for "words" from his/her page to fill in the spaces in the story below. Write the words in the spaces. You may also have the student write these words on his/her Companion Activity Sheet (page 29). Then, have the student read/listen to the story. For more options, see *How To Use This Book* on page ii.

Ladies and gentlemen, boys and girls!. May I call your attention to the Ring Toss? If

you can throw three rings around the _____, or if you throw four around the
(regular plural)

_____, you can win this large adorable doll. If you win more than once, you
(regular plural)

can even take your large doll and trade it for two smaller _____ ! The Dart
(irregular plural)

Throw is in the next booth. You have to throw darts at _____ to win
(irregular plural)

_____ . You have to break more _____ than at the ring toss,
(regular plural)   (irregular plural)

but you win two _____ , so this is a much better deal! At the Softball
(regular plural)

Throw, if you knock down just one pin, it doesn't count. You have to knock down all of the

_____ to win. So ... ladies and gentlemen, boy and girls, step right up !!!
(irregular plural)

Questions: (Answer in a complete sentence.)
- ❏ 1. What will you win at the Ring Toss game?
- ❏ 2. What do you throw the ring/rings around at the Ring Toss game?
- ❏ 3. If you win more than once, what do you get when you trade?
- ❏ 4. What do you throw darts at for the Dart Throw game?
- ❏ 5. What do you have to knock down at the Softball Throw game?

Homework: Take a copy of this Story and Word List home, and follow the Directions above.

_____   _____   _____
Name   Homework Partner   Date

Plurals Combo

#BK-309 Grammar Tickle Stories™ • ©2004 Super Duper® Publications • 1-800-277-8737 • Online! www.superduperinc.com

Funny Putty Golf

Directions: Give each student a list of the Picture Words on pages 2 and 13 or the Word Lists on pages 3 and 14. Do not reveal the story title. Ask each student for "words" from his/her page to fill in the spaces in the story below. Write the words in the spaces. You may also have the student write these words on his/her Companion Activity Sheet (page 29). Then, have the student read/listen to the story. For more options, see *How To Use This Book* on page ii.

This week, *Funny Putty Golf Course* begins construction with lots of new fun

attractions. The first hole will have many _____ surrounded by a lot of little

(regular plural)

_____ and will be pretty easy. The course gets harder at Hole 4, where
(regular plural)

you have to putt the ball around the large _____ . By Hole 6, you'll really

(irregular plural)

be having fun when the _____ pop up and scare you. At the 9th Hole, you

(regular plural)

can rest by the _____ . Then get ready for the challenge! Hole 11 has

(irregular plural)

you go around two very wide _____ . When you get done, you can choose

(regular plural)

a prize, like some _____ or some _____ . Get ready for

(irregular plural)   (irregular plural)

Tee Time!

Questions: (Answer in a complete sentence.)

❏ 1. What will be at the first hole?

❏ 2. What will you putt around at hole 4?

❏ 3. What will scare you at hole 6?

❏ 4. What can you rest by at hole 9?

❏ 5. What prizes can you choose from when you're done?

Homework: Take a copy of this story and word/picture list home, and follow the directions above.

Name	Homework Partner	Date	**Plurals Combo**

Party Bags

Directions: Give each student a list of the Picture Words on pages 2 and 13 or the Word Lists on pages 3 and 14. Do not reveal the story title. Ask each student for "words" from his/her page to fill in the spaces in the story below. Write the words in the spaces. You may also have the student write these words on his/her Companion Activity Sheet (page 29). Then, have the student read/listen to the story. For more options, see *How To Use This Book* on page ii.

When you give a party, it's nice to send your guests home with a party bag. Imagine

the joy on their faces when they reach in and pull out some _____. When
                                                                  (regular plural)

choosing your gifts, keep in mind that while some friends may be happy with

_____, others will like a pair of _____. Good places to look
    (irregular plural)   (irregular plural)

for party gifts are stores that sell _____ , where they will usually have at
                                          (regular plural)

least a dozen _____. Here is something to keep in mind. What would you
                   (regular plural)

like to find in a party bag, _____ or _____? If **you'd** like
                                  (regular plural)   (irregular plural)

them, your friends probably would too. So, go plan your party bag today. You'll love

hearing your friends shout, "Look, I got _____ !"
                                              (irregular plural)

Questions: (Answer in a complete sentence.)

❑ 1. What might your friends pull out of the party bag?

❑ 2. What might your friends be happy with just one or a pair of?

❑ 3. What kind of stores are good places to look for party gifts?

❑ 4. What would you like to find in your party bag?

❑ 5. What will your friends shout?

Homework: Take a copy of this story and word/picture list home, and follow the directions above.

_____   _____   _____

Name   Homework Partner   Date

Plurals Combo

#BK-309 Grammar Tickle Stories™ • ©2004 Super Duper® Publications • 1-800-277-8737 • Online! www.superduperinc.com

Choosing a Present for the New Baby

Directions: Give each student a list of the Picture Words on pages 2 and 13 or the Word Lists on pages 3 and 14. Do not reveal the story title. Ask each student for "words" from his/her page to fill in the spaces in the story below. Write the words in the spaces. You may also have the student write these words on his/her Companion Activity Sheet (page 29). Then, have the student read/listen to the story. For more options, see *How To Use This Book* on page ii.

Choosing a present for a new baby is always a challenge! Most moms want some

_____, but say they can never have enough _____. If you
(regular plural)   (regular plural)

are going to a baby shower, you might want to ask if the mother-to-be already has

_____. At the hospital, people often give the new mother a bag containing
(irregular plural)

bright pink or blue _____. Often times babies are too young for
(regular plural)

_____, so getting several _____ is out of the question!
(irregular plural)   (irregular plural)

Babies like bright things. So, if you get outfits, they might have bright orange

_____ on them.   Soft and cuddly _____ are a nice start to a
(regular plural)   (irregular plural)

stuffed toy collection.

Questions: (Answer in a complete sentence.)

❏ 1. What does a new mom want?

❏ 2. If you're going to a baby shower, what should you ask?

❏ 3. What do they give new moms at the hospital?

❏ 4. What looks cute on an outfit for a newborn baby?

❏ 5. What are soft and cuddly and a nice start to a collection?

Homework: Take a copy of this story and word/picture list home, and follow the directions above.

_____   _____   _____
Name   Homework Partner   Date

Plurals Combo

Action Auction

Directions: Give each student a list of the Picture Words on pages 2 and 13 or the Word Lists on pages 3 and 14. Do not reveal the story title. Ask each student for "words" from his/her page to fill in the spaces in the story below. Write the words in the spaces. You may also have the student write these words on his/her Companion Activity Sheet (page 29). Then, have the student read/listen to the story. For more options, see *How To Use This Book* on page ii.

Welcome to our annual Action Auction! The money we raise today will buy new

_____. Our first items were owned by King George the Fourth, who had a
　　(regular plural)

collection of _____. We're lucky to have them in our auction today! Our
　　　　　　(irregular plural)

next items, the adorable _____, will be a great conversation piece in your
　　　　　　　　(regular plural)

home! When you came in, you passed large _____ in the hall. Well, we
　　　　　　　　　　　　(irregular plural)

have a whole caseload of _____ behind the stage! Did you know your
　　　　　　　　(irregular plural)

school principal is donating his _____ from his collection of
　　　　　　　　　(regular plural)

_____, that he got on an African Safari? If you stay until the end, you can
(regular plural)

bid on our prize _____. Now, who will start the bidding?
　　　　(irregular plural)

Questions: (Answer in a complete sentence.)

❏ 1. What will the school buy with the money they raise?

❏ 2. What were the first items up for bid?

❏ 3. What did you pass in the hall, and what is behind the stage?

❏ 4. What is the principal donating, and what is his collection?

❏ 5. What can you bid on at the end?

Homework: Take a copy of this story and word/picture list home, and follow the directions above.

_____　　_____　　_____
　　　　　Name　　　　　　　　　　　　　Homework Partner　　　　　　　Date

Plurals Combo

#BK-309 Grammar Tickle Stories™ • ©2004 Super Duper® Publications • 1-800-277-8737 • Online! www.superduperinc.com

Plurals Combo Companion Activity Sheet

Directions: During or following the story, have the student write words from the word or picture list on the lines below. Then, have the student write sentences with these words in them.

Example: _____*cats*_____ - OR - _____*mice*_____

The **cats** are playing with toys.   The three hungry **mice** are eating cheese.

1. _____   _____

    _____

2. _____   _____

    _____

3. _____   _____

    _____

4. _____   _____

    _____

5. _____   _____

    _____

6. _____   _____

    _____

7. _____   _____

    _____

8. _____   _____

    _____

Homework: Take a copy of this sheet home with a word/picture list. Then, follow the directions above.

_____   _____   _____

Name   Homework Partner   Date

Plurals Combo

More Than One

Directions: Say the word of the picture on the left and match it with it's plural on the right. Say both words.

house

goose

child

tooth

bird

leaf

teeth

leaves

houses

birds

children

geese

Homework: ❏ Use the word pairs in your own sentences.

❏ _____ .

_____   _____   _____
Name   Homework Partner   Date

#BK-309 Grammar Tickle Stories™ • ©2004 Super Duper® Publications • 1-800-277-8737 • Online! www.superduperinc.com

Plural Combo

Look in the mirror and smile! Tell your homework partner what you see using both forms of the word "tooth".

Name _____

Date _____

Plural Combo

Talk about where your shoes go on your body. Tell what you do when you put your shoes on one at a time, and then both together.

Name _____

Date _____

Plural Combo

Find something you have more than one of in your closet. Tell your homework partner: I see one _____, but I have many _____.

Name _____

Date _____

Plural Combo

Go to the place where you keep your toys. Describe one of them. Then, tell your homework partner something about all of them.

Name _____

Date _____

Plurals Combo

Plural Combo

Find something you have more than one of in your drawer. Tell your homework partner: I see one _____, but I have many _____.

Name _____ Date _____

Plural Combo

Find something you have more than one of in your yard. Tell your homework partner: I see one _____, but I have many _____.

Name _____ Date _____

Plural Combo

Talk about a "pet" that would swim in a bowl. Talk about what you would name it, using the sentence, "If I had one _____..." Then, tell what you would name them if you had two _____.

Name _____ Date _____

Plural Combo

Finish these irregular plural pairs:

one man, two _____

one mouse, two _____

one sheep, two _____

one shelf, two _____

Name _____ Date _____

Plurals Combo

#BK-309 Grammar Tickle Stories™ • ©2004 Super Duper® Publications • 1-800-277-8737 • Online! www.superduperinc.com

Possessives

Possessives

Directions: Use the picture words below to help you complete the stories on pages 36 to 40.

alien's

children's

doctor's

painter's

baby's

clown's

dog's

pitcher's

bird's

coach's

drummer's

skater's

boy's

cook's

farmer's

spider's

captain's

cow's

girl's

surfer's

cat's

dad's

firefighter's

teacher's

Possessives

#BK-309 Grammar Tickle Stories™ • ©2004 Super Duper® Publications • 1-800-277-8737 • Online! www.superduperinc.com

Possessives

Directions: Use these words to help complete the stories on pages 36 to 40.

- acrobat's
- actor's
- alien's
- ant's
- artist's
- astronaut's
- baby's
- babysitter's
- barber's
- baseball player's
- bear's
- bird's
- bowler's
- boxer's
- boy's
- brother's
- bull's
- camel's
- camper's
- captain's
- car's
- cat's
- chicken's
- child's
- children's
- clown's
- coach's
- cook's
- cousin's
- cowboy's
- cow's
- crossing guard's
- dad's
- deer's
- director's
- doctor's
- dog's

- drummer's
- duck's
- elephant's
- farmer's
- firefighter's
- fly's
- friend's
- frog's
- giraffe's
- girl's
- golfer's
- gopher's
- grandfather's
- grandmother's
- gymnast's
- hamster's
- hippo's
- horse's
- ice skater's
- jogger's
- librarian's
- lifeguard's
- lion's
- magician's
- mail carrier's
- mom's
- monkey's
- mouse's
- movie star's
- musician's
- painter's
- piano teacher's
- pilot's
- pitcher's
- president's
- principal's
- puppy's

- rabbit's
- scarecrow's
- scientist's
- singer's
- sister's
- skateboard's
- skier's
- skydiver's
- skater's
- snake's
- snowman's
- spider's
- Statue of Liberty's
- surfer's
- teacher's
- team's
- tiger's
- turkey's
- turtle's
- uncle's
- waiter's
- writer's
- zebra's
- zookeeper's

Possessives

Whose Shoes?

Directions: Give each student a list of the Picture Words on page 34 or the Word List on page 35. Do not reveal the story title. Ask each student for "words" from his/her page to fill in the spaces in the story below. Write the words in the spaces. You may also have the student write these words on his/her Companion Activity Sheet (page 41). Then, have the student read/listen to the story. For more options, see *How To Use This Book* on page ii.

Lost and Found

It's time to clear out the _____ *Lost and Found Department*.

(possessive)

1. We have a pair of running shoes like the _____ shoes, except they're

(possessive)

blue. The coach thinks they might be the _____ shoes. If you know anything

(possessive)

about these, please contact Coach Fouler.

2. This large black backpack could be the _____, but it's very heavy.

(possessive)

There's a week old lunch in it that I think we can safely say is the _____

(possessive)

lunch! Please, come remove this immediately!

3. A red baseball hat was left on the playground. Our principal, Mr. Fuddernut, thinks

it's the _____ hat. From the logo on it, it could also be the

(possessive)

_____ hat.

(possessive)

Mr. Fuddernut wants all items in the *Lost and Found* gone by the end of

the day. Whatever isn't claimed will become the _____ property. Yikes!

(possessive)

Questions: (Answer in a complete sentence.)
- ❑ 1. What does the announcement say about who or what the shoes might belong to?
- ❑ 2. What does the announcement say about who or what the backpack might belong to?
- ❑ 3. What does the announcement say about who or what the lunch belongs to?
- ❑ 4. What does the announcement say about who or what Mr. Fuddernut thinks the hat belongs to?
- ❑ 5. If the things aren't claimed, whose property will they become?

Homework: Take a copy of this story and word/picture list home, and follow the directions above.

_____   _____   _____

Name   Homework Partner   Date   **Possessives**

#BK-309 Grammar Tickle Stories™ • ©2004 Super Duper® Publications • 1-800-277-8737 • Online! www.superduperinc.com

Kittens and Mittens

Directions: Give each student a list of the Picture Words on page 34 or the Word List on page 35. Do not reveal the story title. Ask each student for "words" from his/her page to fill in the spaces in the story below. Write the words in the spaces. You may also have the student write these words on his/her Companion Activity Sheet (page 41). Then, have the student read/listen to the story. For more options, see *How To Use This Book* on page ii.

The three little kittens have lost their mittens and don't know where to find them.

These mittens used to be the _____ mittens, but they were given to the
(possessive)

kittens as a gift. They used to wear the _____ gloves and the
(possessive)

_____ hats until they got their own. The kittens discovered they were
(possessive)

missing while they were eating the _____ cheese, and it got all over their
(possessive)

paws! They went to wash up with the _____ soap and noticed...no gloves!
(possessive)

Their mother scolded them and said they couldn't have any of the _____
(possessive)

pie for dessert. This made them cry. Then, they looked under the _____
(possessive)

bed and there they were! The kittens had been playing with the _____ toys.
(possessive)

They had taken off their gloves and left them there! Mommy Cat hugged them, and they

all had pie with their mittens on!

Questions: (Answer in a complete sentence.)
- ❏ 1. Who did the mittens belong to before they were given to the kittens?
- ❏ 2. Whose gloves and hats did the kittens used to wear?
- ❏ 3. Whose cheese were the kittens eating?
- ❏ 4. Whose soap did the kittens wash with?
- ❏ 5. Whose toys were the kittens playing with when they took off their gloves?

Homework: Take a copy of this story and word/picture list home, and follow the directions above.

_____   _____   _____   **Possessives**
Name   Homework Partner   Date

Papa Bear Bears All

Directions: Give each student a list of the Picture Words on page 34 or the Word List on page 35. Do not reveal the story title. Ask each student for "words" from his/her page to fill in the spaces in the story below. Write the words in the spaces. You may also have the student write these words on his/her Companion Activity Sheet (page 41). Then, have the student read/listen to the story. For more options, see *How To Use This Book* on page ii.

GRRRRRRR....I came home from a nice walk in the woods one day and what did I

see? I saw the _____ porridge on the table all cold, and the
                          (possessive)

_____ porridge was all gone. So, I went over to the chairs and I saw the
(possessive)

_____ chair was out of place. I straightened it when I noticed, from behind
(possessive)

the little table, that the _____ chair was broken into bits. I saw something
                               (possessive)

suspicious, so I went on up the stairs, and there was the _____ bed, kind
                                                              (possessive)

of rumpled up. I looked over at the _____ bed, and I saw a little girl sound
                                         (possessive)

asleep and snoring.   Just as I went over to her, she woke up and started screaming! I

said, "This is the _____ home. What are you doing here?" She ran away
                      (possessive)

so fast, I couldn't offer her any of the _____ warm muffins. Gee, I hope
                                            (possessive)

she comes back some day!

Questions: (Answer in a complete sentence.)
- ❏ 1. Whose cold porridge did Papa Bear see on the table?
- ❏ 2. Whose chair was out of place?
- ❏ 3. Whose chair is broken?
- ❏ 4. Whose bed is rumpled?
- ❏ 5. Whose muffins did Papa Bear want to offer to the visitor?

Homework: Take a copy of this story and word/picture list home, and follow the directions above.

_____   _____   _____ | **Possessives** |
Name   Homework Partner   Date

A Million Excuses

Directions: Give each student a list of the Picture Words on page 34 or the Word List on page 35. Do not reveal the story title. Ask each student for "words" from his/her page to fill in the spaces in the story below. Write the words in the spaces. You may also have the student write these words on his/her Companion Activity Sheet (page 41). Then, have the student read/listen to the story. For more options, see *How To Use This Book* on page ii.

Our teacher, Mrs. Noway, said that she's heard every excuse in the book for a student

fogetting their homework. Here are her favorites:

1. It was the _____ fault because she thought it was a noodle casserole
   (possessive)
   and ate it.

2. It was the _____ idea to make it into a paper plane and try and fly it.
   (possessive)

3. It was the _____ turn to kill a spider, so he used my homework to do it.
   (possessive)

4. I was coming back from the _____ house and a gust of wind blew it away.
   (possessive)

5. I saw the _____ spaceship and before I could run, aliens took it from me.
   (possessive)

6. I dreamt I was having dinner at the _____ house, and when I woke up my
   (possessive)
   homework was mysteriously covered in ketchup.

7. I accidentally put my homework in the _____ backpack and it disappeared.
   (possessive)

Well, after I heard this list, I was too afraid to tell my teacher that it was the _____

(possessive)

fault. So, I have to go home now and redo my homework.

Questions: (Answer in a complete sentence.)
- ❑ 1. Whose fault was it in #1?
- ❑ 2. Whose idea was it to make a paper plane out of the homework?
- ❑ 3. Whose turn was it to kill the spider?
- ❑ 4. Whose spaceship landed?
- ❑ 5. Whose backpack did the homework accidentally get into?

Homework: Take a copy of this story and word/picture list home, and follow the directions above.

| Name | Homework Partner | Date | **Possessives** |

It's in the Bag

Directions: Give each student a list of the Picture Words on page 34 or the Word List on page 35. Do not reveal the story title. Ask each student for "words" from his/her page to fill in the spaces in the story below. Write the words in the spaces. You may also have the student write these words on his/her Companion Activity Sheet (page 41). Then, have the student read/listen to the story. For more options, see *How To Use This Book* on page ii.

"Today class, we're going to have a guessing lesson called *What's in the Bag*?," said

the teacher. I've brought an item in a paper sack. You can put your hand in, but don't look!

"Oh, I bet it's the _____ stapler," shouted Johnny Jones.
(possessive)

"Is it the_____ pencil?" asked Mary Sue Sutton.
(possessive)

"It feels like the_____ scrub brush," said Janie Jansson.
(possessive)

"Remember, last week we had the _____ radio, and the _____
(possessive)   (possessive)

calculator the week before, so don't guess those," warned the teacher. "Could it be the

_____ lost shoes?" asked Pammy Peters.
(possessive)

"Actually, this used to be the_____," said the teacher, "but now it's mine!"
(possessive)

She pulled out a beautiful, antique wooden hairbrush. It even had the _____
(possessive)

initials on it! Our teacher let us look at it and then put it back into the bag.

Questions: (Answer in a complete sentence.)
- ❏ 1. Whose stapler did Johnny guess it was?
- ❏ 2. Whose scrub brush did Janie think it was?
- ❏ 3. Whose radio was in the bag last week?
- ❏ 4. Whose lost shoe did Pammy Peters think it was?
- ❏ 5. Whose initials were on the hairbrush?

Homework: Take a copy of this story and word/picture list home, and follow the directions above.

_____ _____ _____   **Possessives**
Name   Homework Partner   Date

Possessives Companion Activity Sheet

Directions: During or following the story, have the student write words from the word or picture list on the lines below. Then, have the student write sentences with these words in them.

Example: _____ **clown's** _____

The **clown's** costume is very colorful.

1. _____

_____

2. _____

_____

3. _____

_____

4. _____

_____

5. _____

_____

6. _____

_____

7. _____

_____

8. _____

_____

Homework: Take a copy of this sheet home with a word/picture list. Then, follow the directions.

| Name | Homework Partner | Date | **Possessives** |

A Sense of Belonging

Directions: Read the description sentence on the left. Find the picture object on the right that goes with it. Draw a line to the sentence. Then, tell what items belong using the possessive form, i.e. This is the boy's cap.

1. The shoes belong to the runner.

the kittens'

2. The red baseball cap belongs to the boy.

the girl's

3. The mittens belong to the kittens.

the bears'

4. The porridge belongs to the three bears.

the runner's

5. The stapler belongs to the teacher.

the boy's

6. The homework belongs to the girl.

the teacher's

Homework: ❑ Say each possessive form in your own sentence.

❑ _____.

_____	_____	_____
Name	Homework Partner	Date

Possessives

#BK-309 Grammar Tickle Stories™ • ©2004 Super Duper® Publications • 1-800-277-8737 • Online! www.superduperinc.com

Possessives

Tell your homework partner in a complete sentence:

1. Whose slippers are in mom's closet?

2. The shoes belong to mom. Whose shoes are they?

_____ Name

_____ Date

Possessives

Tell your homework partner in a complete sentence:

1. Whose shirt is in dad's closet?

2. The pants belong to dad. Whose pants are they?

_____ Name

_____ Date

Possessives

Tell your homework partner in a complete sentence:

1. Whose newspaper is on the neighbor's driveway?

2. The car in the garage next door belongs to the neighbor. Whose car is it?

_____ Name

_____ Date

Possessives

Tell your homework partner in a complete sentence:

1. In whose truck does the mailman deliver the mail?

2. The mailbag belongs to the mailman. Whose mailbag is it?

_____ Name

_____ Date

Possessives

Possessives

Tell your homework partner in a complete sentence:

Change this description to a possessive to tell who owns an item:

1. The bat belongs to the boy.

   It's the _____ bat.

2. The bike belongs to the girl.

   It's the _____ bike.

_____ _____
Name   Date

Possessives

Tell your homework partner in a complete sentence:

Change this description to a possessive to tell who owns an item:

1. The worm that belongs to the bird.

   It's the _____ worm.

2. The web that belongs to the spider.

   It's the _____ web.

_____ _____
Name   Date

Possessives

Tell your homework partner in a complete sentence:

1. Whose truck picks up the garbage?

2. The garbage can belongs to the garbage man. Whose garbage can is it?

_____ _____
Name   Date

Possessives

Tell your homework partner in a complete sentence:

Change this description to a possessive to tell who owns the item:

1. The bone that belongs to the dog.

   It's the _____ bone.

2. The toy that belongs to the cat.

   It's the _____ toy.

_____ _____
Name   Date

Possessives

44

Prepositional Phrases

Prepositional Phrases

Directions: Use the picture words below to help you complete the stories on pages 48 to 52.

at the pool

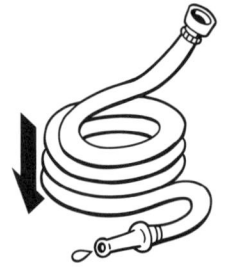

by the hose

near the computer

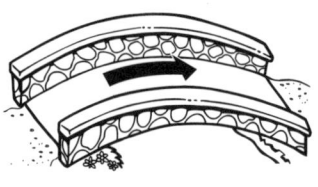

over the bridge

at the store

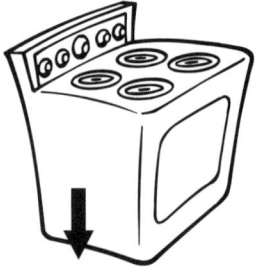

by the stove

near the horse

over the tree

behind the barn

in the trash

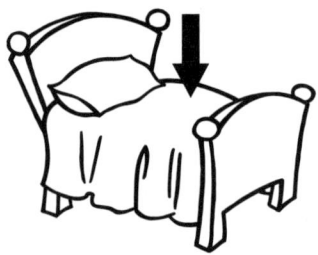

on the bed

under the chair

behind the piano

in the mailbox

on the table

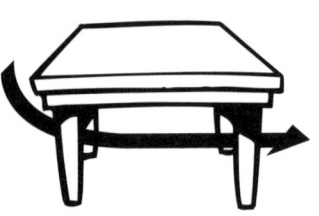

under the table

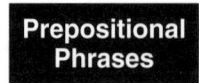

Prepositional Phrases

#BK-309 Grammar Tickle Stories™ • ©2004 Super Duper® Publications • 1-800-277-8737 • Online! www.superduperinc.com

Prepositional Phrases

Directions: Use these words to help complete the stories on pages 48 to 52.

- ❏ across the bridge
- ❏ across the country
- ❏ across the field
- ❏ across the hall
- ❏ across the river
- ❏ across the room
- ❏ across the row
- ❏ across the street
- ❏ across the table
- ❏ across the yard
- ❏ at the beach
- ❏ at the mall
- ❏ at the movies
- ❏ at the park
- ❏ at the pool
- ❏ at the store
- ❏ behind the barn
- ❏ behind the fence
- ❏ behind the garage
- ❏ behind the hill
- ❏ behind the house
- ❏ behind the piano
- ❏ behind the TV
- ❏ below the counter
- ❏ below the shelf
- ❏ below the sink
- ❏ below the towels
- ❏ below the window
- ❏ between the books
- ❏ between the cars
- ❏ between the doors
- ❏ between the flowers
- ❏ between the houses
- ❏ by the car
- ❏ by the door
- ❏ by the garden
- ❏ by the house
- ❏ by the lake

- ❏ by the stove
- ❏ by the window
- ❏ in the class
- ❏ in the garden
- ❏ in the hall
- ❏ in the house
- ❏ in the mailbox
- ❏ in the room
- ❏ in the sky
- ❏ in the street
- ❏ in the yard
- ❏ near the computer
- ❏ near the door
- ❏ near the eggs
- ❏ near the horse
- ❏ near the kite
- ❏ near the lamp
- ❏ near the playground
- ❏ near the rug
- ❏ near the school
- ❏ near the skateboard
- ❏ near the zoo
- ❏ next to the bed
- ❏ next to the bird
- ❏ next to the book
- ❏ next to the cat
- ❏ next to the lamp
- ❏ next to the toys
- ❏ on the counter
- ❏ on the desk
- ❏ on the ground
- ❏ on the porch
- ❏ on the refrigerator
- ❏ on the sign
- ❏ on the table
- ❏ on the tree
- ❏ on the TV
- ❏ over the bed

- ❏ over the bookshelf
- ❏ over the bridge
- ❏ over the clouds
- ❏ over the gate
- ❏ over the mirror
- ❏ over the mountain
- ❏ over the ocean
- ❏ over the river
- ❏ over the roof
- ❏ over the tree
- ❏ through the door
- ❏ through the halls
- ❏ through the house
- ❏ through the store
- ❏ through the town
- ❏ through the tunnel
- ❏ through the water
- ❏ through the window
- ❏ through the woods
- ❏ under the bed
- ❏ under the blanket
- ❏ under the car
- ❏ under the chair
- ❏ under the chicken
- ❏ under the couch
- ❏ under the ground
- ❏ under the table
- ❏ under the tent
- ❏ under the tree

Prepositional Phrases

Doggy in the Window

Directions: Give each student a list of the Picture Words on page 46 or the Word List on page 47. Do not reveal the story title. Ask each student for "words" from his/her page to fill in the spaces in the story below. Write the words in the spaces. You may also have the student write these words on his/her Companion Activity Sheet (page 53). Then, have the student read/listen to the story. For more options, see *How To Use This Book* on page ii.

Do you remember the song, *How Much Is The Doggy In The Window*? I liked it

so much, that I wrote a brand new one called *How Much Is That Doggy*

_____? Here's how it goes:

(prepositional phrase)

How much is that doggy _____?

(prepositional phrase)

He loves chasing birds _____.

(prepositional phrase)

He used to be happy _____,

(prepositional phrase)

But now he sits down _____.

(prepositional phrase)

If you see him, perhaps _____,

(prepositional phrase)

please tell him I miss him and to come home right away!

Questions: (Answer in a complete sentence.)

❑ 1. What is the title of the new song?

❑ 2. What is the first line of the new song?

❑ 3. Where was the doggy chasing birds?

❑ 4. Where did the doggy used to hang out?

❑ 5. Where might you find him?

Homework: Take a copy of this story and word/picture list home, and follow the directions above.

Name	Homework Partner	Date

Prepositional Phrases

#BK-309 Grammar Tickle Stories™ • ©2004 Super Duper® Publications • 1-800-277-8737 • Online! www.superduperinc.com

The Surprise Package

Directions: Give each student a list of the Picture Words on page 46 or the Word List on page 47. Do not reveal the story title. Ask the student for "words" from his/her page to fill in the spaces in the story below. Write the words in the spaces. You may also have the student write these words on his/her Companion Activity Sheet (page 53). Then, have the student read/listen to the story. For more options, see *How To Use This Book* on page ii.

"Dad, we have a surprise for you," yelled Rosie and Mike. "It's hidden and you'll have to find it!"

Dad was very excited. It was Father's Day and the kids had made a special surprise. First, Dad

looked _____, but he only found a spider. "EEK," he screamed.
            (prepositional phrase)

"Is that my surprise?" Rosie laughed and said, "No, try _____."
                                                              (prepositional phrase)

Dad found a note _____ that said, "Look
                    (prepositional phrase)

_____," but when he got there, there was just another note
        (prepositional phrase)

telling him to search _____. Dad went to more and more
                        (prepositional phrase)

places until finally Mike took him _____. Sitting there was the
                                      (prepositional phrase)

best surprise Dad had ever imagined. What do you think the surprise was?

Questions: (Answer in a complete sentence.)

❑ 1. Where did Dad look first?

❑ 2. Where did Rosie tell Dad to look?

❑ 3. Where did the first note tell him to look?

❑ 4. Where did the second note tell him to search?

❑ 5. Where did Mike take him to find his surprise?

Homework: Take a copy of this story and word/picture list home, and follow the directions above.

_____ _____ _____ **Prepositional Phrases**

Name   Homework Partner   Date

Mystery Socks

Directions: Give each student a list of the Picture Words on page 46 or the Word List on page 47. Do not reveal the story title. Ask each student for "words" from his/her page to fill in the spaces in the story below. Write the words in the spaces. You may also have the student write these words on his/her Companion Activity Sheet (page 53). Then, have the student read/listen to the story. For more options, see *How To Use This Book* on page ii.

Have you ever noticed that a pair of socks can go into a washing machine and dryer, but

that often only one sock comes back out? The mystery is, where do socks go? The first time

this happened to me, I looked _____, even though I
                                      (prepositional phrase)

doubted they would go that far. My best friend told me that she heard that missing socks

were _____, but she'd never found any there. I heard a
         (prepositional phrase)

fairy tale that said missing socks can always be found _____.
                                                            (prepositional phrase)

Why they would want to go there is beyond me. I dreamed one night that there was a

beautiful land _____ where socks played all day long. But,
                    (prepositional phrase)

that was just a dream. When I woke up, my socks were _____,
                                                          (prepositional phrase)

just where I'd left them. Do you have any idea where missing socks go?

They always go _____!
                    (prepositional phrase)

Questions: (Answer in a complete sentence.)

❏ 1. Where did the writer look the first time the socks were missing?

❏ 2. Where did the best friend say socks went?

❏ 3. Where did the fairy tale say missing socks could be found?

❏ 4. Where did the writer dream that missing socks were?

❏ 5. Where did the writer find the socks when he or she woke up?

Homework: Take a copy of this story and word/picture list home, and follow the directions above.

| _____ | _____ | _____ |
| Name | Homework Partner | Date |

Prepositional Phrases

#BK-309 Grammar Tickle Stories™ • ©2004 Super Duper® Publications • 1-800-277-8737 • Online! www.superduperinc.com

How (Not) To Diaper A Baby Doll

Directions: Give each student a list of the Picture Words on page 46 or the Word List on page 47. Do not reveal the story title. Ask each student for "words" from his/her page to fill in the spaces in the story below. Write the words in the spaces. You may also have the student write these words on his/her Companion Activity Sheet (page 53). Then, have the student read/listen to the story. For more options, see *How To Use This Book* on page ii.

Here is your first lesson on the correct way to diaper a baby.

Let's use a baby doll for practice. You will know when the baby needs to be changed

by the "change of perfume" in the air! Now, babies don't like to be still, so you may have

to chase the baby _____. Gently pick
(prepositional phrase)

up the doll without squishing the diaper (everyone say "EWWWWWW") and put the doll

_____. This is a good place to change a diaper.
(prepositional phrase)

Next, remove the diaper. Place it _____. Then,
(prepositional phrase)

find a new diaper _____. Gently place the baby
(prepositional phrase)

doll _____ to wash his or her little bottom. Now
(prepositional phrase)

pat dry, powder, and place the baby doll back _____.
(prepositional phrase)

Next lesson: How to pay your baby brother or sister to diaper the baby doll for you.

Questions: (Answer in a complete sentence.)
- ❏ 1. Where might you have to chase the baby?
- ❏ 2. Where should you put the baby to change the diaper?
- ❏ 3. Where should you place the dirty diaper after you remove it?
- ❏ 4. Where will you find a new diaper?
- ❏ 5. Where should you place the baby to wash his or her little bottom?

Homework: Take a copy of this story and word/picture list home, and follow the directions above.

_____   _____   _____
Name   Homework Partner   Date

Prepositional Phrases

Gloom And Dr. Doomy

Directions: Give each student a list of the Picture Words on page 46 or the Word List on page 47. Do not reveal the story title. Ask each student for "words" from his/her page to fill in the spaces in the story below. Write the words in the spaces. You may also have the student write these words on his/her Companion Activity Sheet (page 53). Then, have the student read/listen to the story. For more options, see *How To Use This Book* on page ii.

Tour Guide

Welcome to Castle Gloom! Today, we're going on a tour of a real haunted

house. If you'll step _____, you'll see the
(prepositional phrase)

portrait of Dr. Doomy, the owner of this castle. He liked to spend most of his time

_____, even though he could go into any
(prepositional phrase)

room he wanted. Some people say that they see Dr. Doomy's ghost pacing

_____ on dark foggy nights. We don't
(prepositional phrase)

know for sure, but some people say they see his ghost riding his horse Bullet

_____ on rainy days. So be careful the next
(prepositional phrase)

time you go _____, because that was
(prepositional phrase)

Dr. Doomy's favorite place to mix his magic potions. Anyone care to join me in the

lab-or-a-tory? (evil laugh...heh heh heh)

It's _____.
(prepositional phrase)

Questions: (Answer in a complete sentence.)

❏ 1. Where will you see the portrait of Dr. Doomy?

❏ 2. Where did Dr. Doomy like to spend most of his time?

❏ 3. Where do some people say they see Dr. Doomy's ghost on dark foggy nights?

❏ 4. Where do some people say they see Dr. Doomy riding his horse?

❏ 5. Where is the laboratory?

Homework: Take a copy of this story and word/picture list home, and follow the directions above.

_____ _____ _____ **Prepositional Phrases**

Name   Homework Partner   Date

#BK-309 Grammar Tickle Stories™ • ©2004 Super Duper® Publications • 1-800-277-8737 • Online! www.superduperinc.com

Prepositional Phrases Companion Activity Sheet

Directions: During or following the story, have the student write words from the word or picture list on the lines below. Then, have the student write sentences with these words in them.

Example: _____ ***in the mailbox*** _____

_____ *I found the letter **in the mailbox**.* _____

1. _____

_____

2. _____

_____

3. _____

_____

4. _____

_____

5. _____

_____

6. _____

_____

Homework: ❑ Take a copy of this sheet home with a word/picture list. Then, follow the directions above.

_____ _____ _____   **Prepositional Phrases**
Name   Homework Partner   Date

#BK-309 *Grammar Tickle Stories*™ • ©2004 Super Duper® Publications • 1-800-277-8737 • Online! www.superduperinc.com   53

On A Roll For Fun

Directions: Write the letters "a" through "f" on small cards. Have students roll a die and read the sentence that corresponds to the number on the die. Then, have the student choose a letter card and read the corresponding answer. Enjoy the silly sentences. If a correct match is made, score a point! Game Option: Make a check each time you use a number and letter. The first person to check off all his/her numbers and letters wins!

1. The cute little doggy is sitting

    a. **in** the window.

2. The children's surprise was hiding

    b. **behind** the couch.

3. The missing socks were found

    c. **under** the bed.

4. Put the baby's dirty diaper

    d. **outside** in the trash.

5. Always bathe the baby

    e. **in** the sink.

6. Dr. Doom's laboratory is

    f. **next** to the tower.

Homework: ❏ Say each prepositional phrase in your own sentence.

❏ _____

_____ _____ _____

Name   Homework Partner   Date

Prepositional Phrases

#BK-309 Grammar Tickle Stories™ • ©2004 Super Duper® Publications • 1-800-277-8737 • Online! www.superduperinc.com

Prepositional Phrases

Tell your homework partner in a complete sentence:

1. Where are your socks?

2. What is next to your bed?

_____   _____
Name   Date

Prepositional Phrases

Tell your homework partner in a complete sentence:

1. Where are the pencils?

2. What is behind the couch?

_____   _____
Name   Date

Prepositional Phrases

Tell your homework partner in a complete sentence:

1. Where is the TV?

2. What is parked in the garage?

_____   _____
Name   Date

Prepositional Phrases

Tell your homework partner in a complete sentence:

1. Where is the silverware?

2. What is in the kitchen cupboard?

_____   _____
Name   Date

Prepositional Phrases

Prepositional Phrases

Tell your homework partner in a complete sentence:

1. Where is the telephone?

2. What is under your bed?

Name _____

Date _____

Prepositional Phrases

Tell your homework partner in a complete sentence:

1. Where are your shoes?

2. What is near your dresser?

Name _____

Date _____

Prepositional Phrases

Tell your homework partner in a complete sentence:

1. Where does a picture hang?

2. What is on top of a shelf?

Name _____

Date _____

Prepositional Phrases

Tell your homework partner in a complete sentence:

1. Where would you buy groceries?

2. What do you find at the beach?

Name _____

Date _____

Prepositional Phrases

#BK-309 Grammar Tickle Stories™ • ©2004 Super Duper® Publications • 1-800-277-8737 • Online! www.superduperinc.com

Comparatives and Superlatives

Comparative/Superlative

Directions: Use the picture words below to help you complete the stories on pages 61 to 65 and 70 to 74.

base word	-er	-est
big	bigg**er**	bigg**est**
dirty	dirti**er**	dirti**est**
heavy	heavi**er**	heavi**est**
hot	hott**er**	hott**est**
long	long**er**	long**est**
old	old**er**	old**est**

#BK-309 Grammar Tickle Stories™ • ©2004 Super Duper® Publications • 1-800-277-8737 • Online! www.superduperinc.com

Comparative/Superlative

Directions: Use the picture words below to help you complete the stories on pages 61 to 65 and 70 to 74.

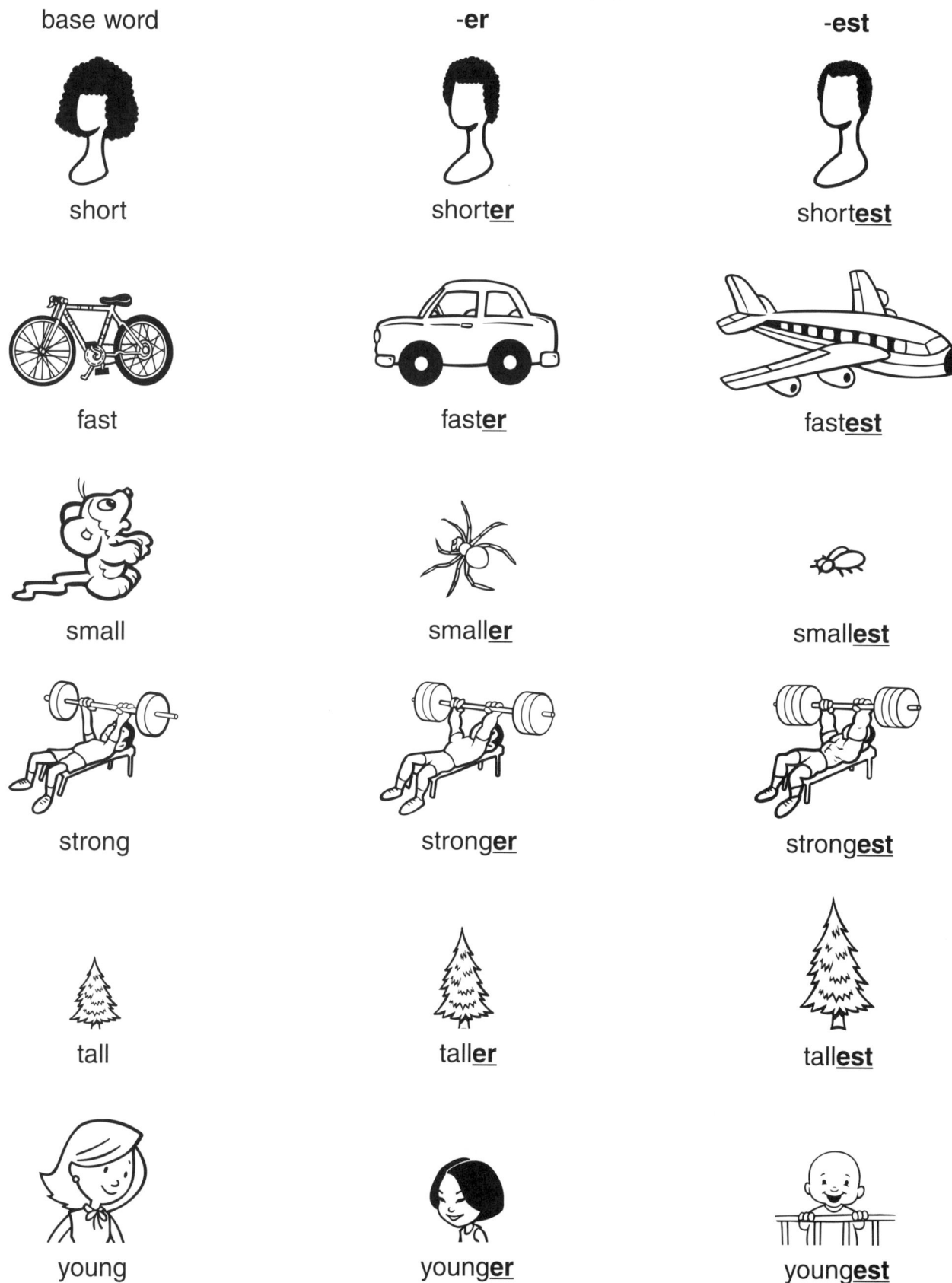

base word	-er	-est
short	short**er**	short**est**
fast	fast**er**	fast**est**
small	small**er**	small**est**
strong	strong**er**	strong**est**
tall	tall**er**	tall**est**
young	young**er**	young**est**

Comparatives

Comparative/Superlative

Directions: Use these words to help complete the stories on pages 61 to 65 and 70 to 74.

BASE	- ER	- EST
❑ big	❑ bigger	❑ biggest
❑ clean	❑ cleaner	❑ cleanest
❑ cold	❑ colder	❑ coldest
❑ cute	❑ cuter	❑ cutest
❑ dirty	❑ dirtier	❑ dirtiest
❑ easy	❑ easier	❑ easiest
❑ far	❑ farther	❑ farthest
❑ fast	❑ faster	❑ fastest
❑ funny	❑ funnier	❑ funniest
❑ happy	❑ happier	❑ happiest
❑ hard	❑ harder	❑ hardest
❑ heavy	❑ heavier	❑ heaviest
❑ high	❑ higher	❑ highest
❑ hot	❑ hotter	❑ hottest
❑ little	❑ littler	❑ littlest
❑ long	❑ longer	❑ longest
❑ loud	❑ louder	❑ loudest
❑ low	❑ lower	❑ lowest
❑ near	❑ nearer	❑ nearest
❑ new	❑ newer	❑ newest
❑ nice	❑ nicer	❑ nicest
❑ old	❑ older	❑ oldest
❑ quiet	❑ quieter	❑ quietest
❑ rich	❑ richer	❑ richest
❑ sad	❑ sadder	❑ saddest
❑ short	❑ shorter	❑ shortest
❑ slow	❑ slower	❑ slowest
❑ small	❑ smaller	❑ smallest
❑ strong	❑ stronger	❑ strongest
❑ sweet	❑ sweeter	❑ sweetest
❑ tall	❑ taller	❑ tallest
❑ weak	❑ weaker	❑ weakest
❑ wet	❑ wetter	❑ wettest
❑ wide	❑ wider	❑ widest
❑ young	❑ younger	❑ youngest

Comparatives

#BK-309 Grammar Tickle Stories™ • ©2004 Super Duper® Publications • 1-800-277-8737 • Online! www.superduperinc.com

Twin Win

Directions: Give each student a list of the Picture Words on pages 58-59 or the Word Lists on page 60. Do not reveal the story title. Ask each student for "words" from his/her page to fill in the spaces in the story below. Write the words in the spaces. You may also have the student write these words on his/her Companion Activity Sheet (page 66). Then, have the student read/listen to the story. For more options, see *How To Use This Book* on page ii.

Introducing New Twin Students to Their Classmates

Hi, I'm Gwen and this is Jen! We're identical twins, but we're going to help you tell

us apart. I'm _____, but Jen is _____. Jen's hair is
　　　　　　　(base word)　　　　　　　　　　　　　　　(er)

_____, but my hair is _____. My eyes are
　　(base word)　　　　　　　　　　　　　　(er)

_____ and Jen's eyes are _____. Sometimes, our parents
　　(base word)　　　　　　　　　　　　　　(er)

pretend they can't tell us apart. Mom will say, "Let's see is it Gwen or Jen who is

_____!" We laugh and say, "Mom, you know Jen is _____!"
　　(base word)　　　　　　　　　　　　　　　　　　　　　　　　(er)

She pretends to be surprised. We try to fool our baby brother and tell him, "Look, Jen is

_____ and I'm _____," when it's the opposite. He's pretty
　　(base word)　　　　　　　　(er)

smart, though, and it's hard to fool him. But, we won't try to fool you!

Questions: (Answer in a complete sentence.)

❑ 1. What is the first thing Gwen says about herself and her twin Jen?

❑ 2. What does Gwen say about her hair and Jen's hair?

❑ 3. What does Gwen say about her eyes and Jen's eyes?

❑ 4. What does their mother say that makes them laugh?

❑ 5. What does Gwen say they tell their baby brother?

Homework: Take a copy of this story and word/picture list home, and follow the directions above.

Name   Homework Partner   Date   **Comparatives**

Shopping For A Car

Directions: Give each student a list of the Picture Words on pages 58-59 or the Word Lists on page 60. Do not reveal the story title. Ask each student for "words" from his/her page to fill in the spaces in the story below. Write the words in the spaces. You may also have the student write these words on his/her Companion Activity Sheet (page 66). Then, have the student read/listen to the story. For more options, see *How To Use This Book* on page ii.

When choosing a new car, there are important things you should look for. Let's

practice using the blue car on my left and the red car on my right. Notice that the color

on the red car is _____, but the blue one is _____. If you kick
               (base word)   (er)

the tires on the blue car, they're _____ but the ones on the red car are
                                        (base word)

_____. Now, try the horns. The blue car horn is _____ and
      (er)   (base word)

the red car horn is _____. When we do a test drive, you'll notice that the
                      (er)

red car is _____ and the blue car is _____. Finally, look at
            (base word)   (er)

the radios! Turn them on. Do you hear that the blue car's radio is _____
                                                    (base word)

and the red car's radio is _____? Ok, so which one would you want to buy?
                    (er)

Questions: (Answer in a complete sentence.)

❏ 1. Tell about the color on the red and blue cars.

❏ 2. Tell about the tires on the red and blue cars.

❏ 3. Tell about the horn on the red and blue cars.

❏ 4. What happens when you drive the red and blue cars.

❏ 5. Tell about the radio in the red and blue cars.

Homework: Take a copy of this story and word/picture list home, and follow the directions above.

Name	Homework Partner	Date

Comparatives

#BK-309 Grammar Tickle Stories™ • ©2004 Super Duper® Publications • 1-800-277-8737 • Online! www.superduperinc.com

The Ice Cream Man Cometh

Directions: Give each student a list of the Picture Words on pages 58-59 or the Word Lists on page 60. Do not reveal the story title. Ask the student for "words" from his/her pages to fill in the spaces in the story below. Write the words in the spaces. You may also have the student write these words on his/her Companion Activity Sheet (page 66). Then, have the student read/listen to the story. For more options, see *How To Use This Book* on page ii.

When you hear that familiar tinkling song playing in your neighborhood, you know

that the ice cream man is coming! But, how do you decide which ice cream to buy? A

popsicle is _____, but an ice cream sandwich is _____.
            (base word)   (er)

Chocolate ice cream is _____, but vanilla is even _____. If
                       (base word)   (er)

you like ice cream on a stick, then an ice cream bar is _____, but a
                                                        (base word)

fudgsicle is much _____. The ice cream man also sells candy. While a
                  (er)

candy bar is _____, ice cream is always _____. Oh, I think I
             (base word)   (er)

hear him now! The music is very _____, but when I really want ice cream,
                                (base word)

my voice is even _____!.
                 (er)

Questions: (Answer in a complete sentence.)

❑ 1. What does this story say about a popsicle and an ice cream sandwich?

❑ 2. What does this story say about chocolate and vanilla ice cream?

❑ 3. What does this story say about ice cream on a stick and a fudgsicle?

❑ 4. What does this story say about candy and ice cream?

❑ 5. What does this story say about the music and the voice of the story teller?

Homework: Take a copy of this story and word/picture list home, and follow the directions above.

_____   _____   _____   **Comparatives**
        Name   Homework Partner   Date

Choosing A School Mascot

Directions: Give each student a list of the Picture Words on pages 58-59 or the Word Lists on page 60. Do not reveal the story title. Ask the student for "words" from his/her pages to fill in the spaces in the story below. Write the words in the spaces. You may also have the student write these words on his/her Companion Activity Sheet (page 66). Then, have the student read/listen to the story. For more options, see *How To Use This Book* on page ii.

Memo: From The Principal

Today we will be choosing a school mascot. You'll be voting between the penguin

and the duck. Here are some things you should consider before making your decision.

First of all, the penguin is _____, but the duck is _____. If

                       (base word)   (er)

you notice how they move, the duck is _____ and the penguin is

                                             (base word)

_____. They both swim, but the penguin is _____ and the

       (er)   (base word)

duck is _____. Both birds love to play! Look at how the duck is

               (er)

_____ like the other ducks, but the penguin is _____ like his

    (base word)   (er)

playmates. So, when you're making your final decision, keep in mind how this bird will

look on your new school t-shirts. The duck is _____ and the penguin is

                                          (base word)

_____, but they are both lovable creatures.

      (er)

Questions: (Answer in a complete sentence.)

❑ 1. What does this story say first about the duck and the penguin?

❑ 2. What does this story say about how the duck and penguin move?

❑ 3. What does this story say about how the duck and the penguin swim?

❑ 4. What does this story say about how the duck and penguin play?

❑ 5. What does this story say you should consider about how the duck and the penguin will look on your school t-shirt?

Homework: Take a copy of this story and word/picture list home, and follow the directions above.

_____   _____   _____ | Comparatives |

        Name   Homework Partner   Date

#BK-309 Grammar Tickle Stories™ • ©2004 Super Duper® Publications • 1-800-277-8737 • Online! www.superduperinc.com

Urgent! Detergent

Directions: Give each student a list of the Picture Words on pages 58-59 or the Word Lists on page 60. Do not reveal the story title. Ask the student for "words" from his/her pages to fill in the spaces in the story below. Write the words in the spaces. You may also have the student write these words on his/her Companion Activity Sheet (page 66). Then, have the student read/listen to the story. For more options, see *How To Use This Book* on page ii.

TV Reporter: Today we're comparing two laundry detergents. I have Mrs. Wishy and Mr. Washy here to help. First, I have Brand A, *Sunshine*, which you see is _____ and Brand B,

(base word)

Lightening, which is _____ . I have two dirty shirts. The blue shirt is

(er)

_____, but this red shirt is _____. So, let's pour in a cup of each

(base word)   (er)

detergent and see which works the best in these two machines. What do you think, Mrs. Wishy?

Mrs. Wishy: I can see that this machine with the red shirt is _____.

(base word)

TV Reporter: Mr. Washy, what do you see?

Mr. Washy: Well, the machine with the blue shirt is _____.

(er)

TV Reporter: After three minutes, we'll take out our shirts and see if the red shirt is

_____ and the blue shirt is _____ or the other way around!

(base word)   (er)

And here it is folks: The red shirt washed in *Sunshine* is _____ but the blue shirt

(base word)

washed in *Lightening* is _____. Any comments, Mrs. Wishy? Mr. Washy?

(er)

Mrs. Wishy and Mr. Washy: Can we say "Hi" to our family back in Pokono?

Questions: (Answer in a complete sentence.)
- ❏ 1. What does the reporter say first about the detergents *Sunshine* and *Lightening*?
- ❏ 2. What does the reporter say first about the two dirty shirts?
- ❏ 3. What do Mrs. Wishy and Mr. Washy say about the washing machines?
- ❏ 4. What does the reporter say we'll find out in three minutes?
- ❏ 5. How do the red and blue shirts actually come out?

Homework: Take a copy of this story and word/picture list home, and follow the directions above.

_____   _____   _____

Name   Homework Partner   Date   **Comparatives**

Comparatives Companion Activity Sheet

Directions: During or following the story, have the student write words from the word or picture list on the lines below. Then, have the student write sentences with these words in them.

Example: _____ **slow** _____   _____ **slower** _____

_____ The turtle is **slow**, but the snail is **slower**. _____

1. _____   _____

   _____

2. _____   _____

   _____

3. _____   _____

   _____

4. _____   _____

   _____

5. _____   _____

   _____

Homework: ❏ Take a copy of this sheet home with a word/picture list. Then, follow the directions above.

_____   _____   _____   **Comparatives**
        Name   Homework Partner   Date

#BK-309 Grammar Tickle Stories™ • ©2004 Super Duper® Publications • 1-800-277-8737 • Online! www.superduperinc.com

How Sweet/Sweeter It Is!

Directions: Say aloud each sentence below. Decide which word goes in each space and write it on the line provided.

Example: How **sweet/sweeter** it is!

1. A bush is **short** but a flower is _____.

2. A ruler is **long** but a yardstick is _____.

3. A glass of milk is **cold** but a popsicle is _____.

4. A kite is **high** but a cloud is _____.

5. A radio is **loud** but a fire engine is _____.

6. A dog is **young** but a puppy is _____.

Homework: ❏ Say each base and comparative (-er) form in your own sentence.

❏ _____.

_____ _____ _____
Name   Homework Partner   Date   **Comparatives**

Comparatives

Answer the questions in a complete sentence using the correct comparative (-er) form.

1. Who is taller, you or your homework helper?

2. Who is shorter, you or your homework helper?

_____ _____
Name   Date

Comparatives

Answer the questions in a complete sentence using the correct comparative (-er) form.

1. Which is harder, your front door or a cardboard box?

2. Which is softer, your pillow or an apple?

_____ _____
Name   Date

Comparatives

Answer the questions in a complete sentence using the correct comparative (-er) form.

1. Which is quieter, a dog or a goldfish?

2. Which is noisier, a parrot or a bunny?

_____ _____
Name   Date

Comparatives

Answer the questions in a complete sentence using the correct comparative (-er) form.

1. Which is thicker, a cracker or a phone book?

2. Which is thinner, a piece of your notebook paper or a magazine?

_____ _____
Name   Date

Comparatives

#BK-309 Grammar Tickle Stories™ • ©2004 Super Duper® Publications • 1-800-277-8737 • Online! www.superduperinc.com

Comparatives

Answer the questions in a complete sentence, using the correct comparative (-er) form.

1. What is bigger, your TV or your stove?

2. What is smaller, your hairbrush or your toothbrush?

Name _____ Date _____

Comparatives

Answer the questions in a complete sentence, using the correct comparative (-er) form.

1. What is warmer, your pajamas or your t-shirt?

2. What is cooler, your jacket or your shorts?

Name _____ Date _____

Comparatives

Answer the questions in a complete sentence, using the correct comparative (-er) form.

1. What is rougher, sandpaper or your desk?

2. What is softer, a brick or sheets?

Name _____ Date _____

Comparatives

Answer the questions in a complete sentence, using the correct comparative (-er) form.

1. What is hotter, your stove or your refrigerator?

2. What is colder, your freezer or your oven?

Name _____ Date _____

Comparatives

Be Careful What You Wish For!

Directions: Give each student a list of the Picture Words on pages 58-59 or the Word Lists on page 60. Do not reveal the story title. Ask the student for "words" from his/her pages to fill in the spaces in the story below. Write the words in the spaces. You may also have the student write these words on his/her Companion Activity Sheet (page 75). Then, have the student read/listen to the story. For more options, see *How To Use This Book* on page ii.

Dear Mom and Dad:

We're standing here at the famous *Wishing Fountain of Wellington*, in Ireland. When

we arrived, the weather was _____ (base word), but today it's _____ (er) and

the report says tomorrow it will be the _____ (est)! This is the third fountain

we've been to. The first one was _____ (base word), and the second one was

_____ (er), but this *Wishing Fountain* is truly the _____ (est) in all of

Ireland! We're getting ready to make a wish. I have a penny that is _____ (base word),

and Aunt Sylvia has one that is even _____ (er). Uncle Milo's penny is the

_____ (est). We heard a legend that once upon a time, three fair maidens lived

here. Princess Sophie was _____ (base word), her sister Alphia was

_____ (er), and the third sister, Gertruda, was the _____ (est). They

each made a wish. Sophia's wish was _____ (base word), Alphia's was

_____ (er), but Gertruda's was _____ (est). She was never seen

again! So we should be careful what we wish for! Hope to see you soon!

Love,

Your son Lucky

Questions: (Answer in a complete sentence.)
- ❏ 1. How did Lucky describe the weather when they arrived?
- ❏ 2. What did Lucky write about the three fountains?
- ❏ 3. How did Lucky describe the three pennies?
- ❏ 4. How did Lucky describe the three sisters?
- ❏ 5. What did Lucky say about the sisters' three wishes?

Homework: Take a copy of this story and word/picture list home, and follow the directions above.

_____   _____   _____

Name   Homework Partner   Date

Comparatives/ Superlatives

#BK-309 Grammar Tickle Stories™ • ©2004 Super Duper® Publications • 1-800-277-8737 • Online! www.superduperinc.com

Jumping Frogs

Directions: Give each student a list of the Picture Words on page 58-59 or the Word Lists on page 60. Do not reveal the story title. Ask the student for "words" from his/her pages to fill in the spaces in the story below. Write the words in the spaces. You may also have the student write these words on his/her Companion Activity Sheet (page 75). Then, have the student read/listen to the story. For more options, see *How To Use This Book* on page ii.

Welcome to the 10th annual *Jumping Frogs of Juniper County* contest! Our three

frogs, Legs, Hip Hop, and Toady, are lined up and ready to go. You'll notice that Toady is

_____, Hip Hop is _____, and Legs is the _____.
     (base word)   (er)   (est)

We aren't sure why our resident veterinarian, Dr. Needles, says that Legs is

_____ and Hip Hop is _____, but Toady is the _____.
   (base word)   (er)   (est)

Legs is owned by Little Johnny Jones, who is _____. Hip Hop is owned
                                        (base word)

by sweet Miss Minnie Smith, who is _____. Toady is owned by old Mr.
                              (er)

Grumpy, who is the _____. There's the whistle and they're off! Oh, look at
                (est)

Hip Hop! He's _____, but along comes Toady who is _____,
         (base word)   (er)

and right now, Legs is the _____. Along the home stretch, it's Hip Hop,
                   (est)

Legs, and Toady. Coming from behind, Hip Hop is _____, Toady is
                                 (base word)

_____, but it's Legs who is the _____ to the finish line! You
   (er)   (est)

might say that it was a hop, skip, and a jump for Legs!

Questions: (Answer in a complete sentence.)
- ❏ 1. At the start line, how were Toady, Hip Hop, and Legs described?
- ❏ 2. What does Dr. Needles say about Legs, Hip Hop, and Toady?
- ❏ 3. What does the story say about the owners of the frogs?
- ❏ 4. How does the race start out for each frog?
- ❏ 5. Describe how the frogs come down the home stretch.

Homework: Take a copy of this story and word/picture list home, and follow the directions above.

_____   _____   _____
Name   Homework Partner   Date

Comparatives/ Superlatives

Teddy Bear Picnic

Directions: Give each student a list of the Picture Words on page 58-59 or the Word Lists on page 60. Do not reveal the story title. Ask the student for "words" from his/her pages to fill in the spaces in the story below. Write the words in the spaces. You may also have the student write these words on his/her Companion Activity Sheet (page 75). Then, have the student read/listen to the story. For more options, see *How To Use This Book* on page ii.

Tomorrow, our class is going on a Teddy Bear Picnic. Yesterday was a _____ (base word)

day and today is even _____ (er), but tomorrow will be the _____ (est) of

all! Remember to bring a teddy bear with you. A _____ (base word) teddy bear is a good

one, and a _____ (er) one would be better, but the _____ (est) one would

be the best choice! You'll want to dress warmly. If you have a jacket that is

_____ (base word), it will work. A _____ (er) one would keep you warm, but the

_____ (est) one would keep you nice and toasty! We'll provide lunch, but bring

something to drink. A _____ (base word) drink will be nice and cold, a _____ (er)

drink will keep you from getting thirsty, and the _____ (est) drink will really quench

your thirst! Bring a snack. It can be a _____ (base word) snack, or one that is

_____ (er), but you will want to bring the _____ (est) one you can.

Remember to pack extra for your bear!

Questions: (Answer in a complete sentence.)
- ❏ 1. What kind of day was it yesterday and what kind of day will it be tomorrow?
- ❏ 2. What kind of teddy bear is better and what would be the best choice?
- ❏ 3. What kind of jacket will work? What kind will keep you warm? What kind will keep you nice and toasty?
- ❏ 4. What kind of drink is nice and cold? What kind will really quench your thirst?
- ❏ 5. What kind of snack will you want to bring?

Homework: Take a copy of this story and word/picture list home, and follow the directions above.

_____   _____   _____

Name   Homework Partner   Date

Comparatives/ Superlatives

#BK-309 Grammar Tickle Stories™ • ©2004 Super Duper® Publications • 1-800-277-8737 • Online! www.superduperinc.com

Judging Art

Directions: Give each student a list of the Picture Words on page 58-59 or the Word Lists on page 60. Do not reveal the story title. Ask the student for "words" from his/her pages to fill in the spaces in the story below. Write the words in the spaces. You may also have the student write these words on his/her Companion Activity Sheet (page 75). Then, have the student read/listen to the story. For more options, see *How To Use This Book* on page ii.

Leonardo Van Monet, art expert, here to tell you about good art. I will demonstrate

using the famous picture, *The Three Trees.* You'll see that the first tree is

_____, the second tree is _____, and the third tree is the
(base word)   (er)

_____. It's magnificent, isn't it? Under the tree are three squirrels. The
(est)

squirrel on the left is _____, the middle one is _____, and
(base word)   (er)

the one on the right is the _____. Adorable! There are three clouds in the
(est)

sky. That top one is the _____ and the one over the trees is
(base word)

_____. That far one is the _____ of all. It practically floats
(er)   (est)

off the page. Let's look at the birds. The bird in the nest is _____. The
(base word)

one flying is _____. The one on the ground is the _____.
(er)   (est)

Finally, there are three children playing. The young boy is _____ and the
(base word)

girl is _____, but that little baby is the _____ of all. And that
(er)   (est)

folks, makes good art.

Questions: (Answer in a complete sentence.)
- ❏ 1. What does the art expert say about the three trees?
- ❏ 2. What does the art expert say about the three squirrels?
- ❏ 3. What does the art expert say about the three clouds?
- ❏ 4. What does the art expert say about the three birds?
- ❏ 5. What does the art expert say about the three children?

Homework: Take a copy of this story and word/picture list home, and follow the directions above.

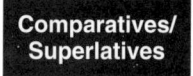

_____ _____ _____
Name   Homework Partner   Date

Comparatives/ Superlatives

Quiz Shows

Directions: Give each student a list of the Picture Words on page 58-59 or the Word Lists on page 60. Do not reveal the story title. Ask the student for "words" from his/her page to fill in the spaces in the story below. Write the words in the spaces. You may also have the student write these words on his/her Companion Activity Sheet (page 75). Then, have the student read/listen to the story. For more options, see *How To Use This Book* on page ii.

Have you ever watched a quiz show? I like the one where you choose a prize behind a

door. If you choose Door Number One, your prize is _____. The Door Number
(base word)

Two prize is _____ and the Door Number Three prize is the _____
(er)   (est)

prize of all. On another show, you get to choose a key to start a car. The bronze key is

_____, the silver key is _____, and the gold key is the
(base word)   (er)

_____. Just like the Olympics, where the bronze medal is _____,
(est)   (base word)

the silver medal is _____, and the gold medal is the _____. I like
(er)   (est)

trivia quiz shows too. The questions for 100 points are _____, for 300 points are
(base word)

_____, and the ones for 600 points are _____ of all! If I were on a
(er)   (est)

quiz show, I'd want to win a trip. A trip to the zoo would be _____, a Disneyland
(base word)

trip would be _____, but a trip to Hawaii would be the _____ of all!
(er)   (est)

What would you want to win on a quiz show?

Questions: (Answer in a complete sentence.)
❏ 1. Tell about the prizes behind the three doors.
❏ 2. Tell about the three car keys.
❏ 3. Tell about the three Olympic medals.
❏ 4. Tell about the trivia quiz show questions.
❏ 5. Tell about the three trips you could win on a quiz show.

Homework: Take a copy of this story and word/picture list home, and follow the directions above.

Comparatives/
Superlatives

_____   _____   _____
Name   Homework Partner   Date

#BK-309 Grammar Tickle Stories™ • ©2004 Super Duper® Publications • 1-800-277-8737 • Online! www.superduperinc.com

Comparatives/Superlatives Companion Activity Sheet

Directions: During or following the story, have the student write words from the word or picture list on the lines below. Then, have the student write sentences with these words in them.

Example: ***big***   ***bigger***   ***biggest***

*A dog is **big,** a horse is **bigger,** and an elephant is the **biggest** animal.*

1.

2.

3.

4.

5.

Homework: ❑ Take a copy of this sheet home with a word/picture list. Then, follow the directions above.

Name   Homework Partner   Date   **Comparatives/ Superlatives**

The Easiest Homework You'll Ever Do!

Directions: Read the words next to each number. Decide which word goes in each sentence and write it on the line.

1. **big/biggest/bigger**

   Baby bear is _____, but Mama Bear is _____, and Papa Bear is the

   _____ of all!

2. **best/better/good**

   Third place is _____, second place is even _____, and first place is the

   _____ of all.

3. **older/old/oldest**

   A boy is _____, but his father is _____, and his grandfather is the

   _____ in the family!

4. **tallest/taller/tall**

   A tree is _____, a skyscraper is _____, but a mountain is the

   _____ of them all!

5. **smaller/small/smallest**

   A mouse is _____ and a spider is even _____, but an ant is the

   _____ of all of them!

Homework: ❏ Say each base, comparative (-er), and superlative (-est) forms in your own sentence.

❏ _____

_____ _____ _____ | Comparatives/ Superlatives |

Name   Homework Partner   Date

#BK-309 Grammar Tickle Stories™ • ©2004 Super Duper® Publications • 1-800-277-8737 • Online! www.superduperinc.com

Superlatives

Answer each question in a complete sentence. Use the correct superlative (-est) form.

1. In your family, who is the tallest?

2. In your family, who is the shortest?

_____   _____
Name   Date

Superlatives

Answer each question in a complete sentence. Use the correct superlative (-est) form.

1. In your family, who is the quietest?

2. In your family, who is the noisiest?

_____   _____
Name   Date

Superlatives

Answer each question in a complete sentence. Use the correct superlative (-est) form.

1. In your house, which room is the quietest?

2. In your house, which room is the noisiest?

_____   _____
Name   Date

Superlatives

Answer each question in a complete sentence. Use the correct superlative (-est) form.

1. In your kitchen, which appliance is the coldest?

2. In your kitchen, which appliance is the hottest?

_____   _____
Name   Date

Comparatives/ Superlatives

Superlatives

Answer each question in a complete sentence. Use the correct superlative (-est) form.

1. In your house, what furniture is the heaviest?

2. In your house, what furniture is the lightest?

Name _____

Date _____

Superlatives

Answer each question in a complete sentence. Use the correct superlative (-est) form.

1. Of all your shirts, which do you like the best?

2. Of all your shirts, which do you like the least?

Name _____

Date _____

Superlatives

Answer each question in a complete sentence. Use the correct superlative (-est) form.

1. In your house, which room is the biggest?

2. In your house, which room is the smallest?

Name _____

Date _____

Superlatives

Answer each question in a complete sentence. Use the correct superlative (-est) form.

1. In your closet, which shoes are the newest?

2. In your closet, which shoes are the oldest?

Name _____

Date _____

Comparatives/ Superlatives

Is and Are
Verb+ing

Is Verb+ing

Directions: Use the picture words below to help you complete the stories on pages 82 to 86 and 102 to 106.

is baking

is crawling

is eating

is reading

is barking

is crying

is fishing

is sewing

is brushing

is cutting

is jumping

is sleeping

is building

is digging

is kicking

is swimming

is clapping

is drinking

is laughing

is throwing

is climbing

is driving

is painting

is writing

Is Verb+ing

#BK-309 Grammar Tickle Stories™ • ©2004 Super Duper® Publications • 1-800-277-8737 • Online! www.superduperinc.com

Is Verb+ing

Directions: Use these words to help complete the stories on pages 82 to 86 and 102 to 106.

❏ is acting	❏ is giggling	❏ is running
❏ is asking	❏ is giving	❏ is sailing
❏ is baking	❏ is growing	❏ is sewing
❏ is barking	❏ is helping	❏ is shopping
❏ is breaking	❏ is hiding	❏ is singing
❏ is brushing	❏ is hiking	❏ is sitting
❏ is buying	❏ is holding	❏ is skating
❏ is calling	❏ is hopping	❏ is skiing
❏ is carrying	❏ is hugging	❏ is sleeping
❏ is catching	❏ is jumping	❏ is sliding
❏ is chasing	❏ is keeping	❏ is smelling
❏ is clapping	❏ is kissing	❏ is smiling
❏ is cleaning	❏ is laughing	❏ is sneezing
❏ is climbing	❏ is leaving	❏ is speaking
❏ is combing	❏ is listening	❏ is spilling
❏ is cooking	❏ is looking	❏ is splashing
❏ is counting	❏ is mailing	❏ is standing
❏ is crawling	❏ is mopping	❏ is studying
❏ is crying	❏ is mowing	❏ is swimming
❏ is cutting	❏ is opening	❏ is swinging
❏ is dancing	❏ is painting	❏ is talking
❏ is daydreaming	❏ is pasting	❏ is thinking
❏ is digging	❏ is petting	❏ is throwing
❏ is drawing	❏ is planting	❏ is tearing
❏ is drinking	❏ is playing	❏ is thanking
❏ is driving	❏ is pouring	❏ is tickling
❏ is dusting	❏ is pulling	❏ is walking
❏ is eating	❏ is racing	❏ is watching
❏ is exercising	❏ is raining	❏ is waving
❏ is falling	❏ is raking	❏ is wearing
❏ is fishing	❏ is reading	❏ is whistling
❏ is fixing	❏ is resting	❏ is wishing
❏ is flying	❏ is riding	❏ is writing
❏ is folding	❏ is ringing	❏ is yelling

Is Verb+ing

A Happy Day

Directions: Give each student a list of the Picture Words on page 80 or the Word List on page 81. Do not reveal the story title. Ask each student for "words" from his/her page to fill in the spaces in the story below. Write the words in the spaces. You may also have the student write these words on his/her Companion Activity Sheet (page 87). Then, have the student read/listen to the story. For more options, see *How To Use This Book* on page ii.

"Hurry, Mom, Happy _____!" yelled Jane. Mom rushed to
(is verb+ing)

the window to see the puppy. "Oh look, the neighbor, Mrs. Johnson,

_____ and Happy likes it," said Jane. I can tell because Happy
(is verb+ing)

_____ right now! The paper boy threw the paper on the lawn.
(is verb+ing)

"Look, the paper boy _____ and Happy likes it!" said Mom. "I
(is verb+ing)

can tell because Happy _____ right now!" Dad came to the
(is verb+ing)

window. "Oh, I see, Happy _____ on the lawn!" They all yelled
(is verb+ing)

out the window, "Happy? Oh Happy!" Happy stopped and looked up. "Now Happy

_____!" said Jane. Jane called to Happy again. They went into the
(is verb+ing)

house. "Now Happy _____ happily in the corner," said Dad. "I
(is verb+ing)

guess you could say that this has been a Happy day!"

Questions: (Answer in a complete sentence.)

❏ 1. Jane tells Mom to hurry to the window. What is Happy doing?

❏ 2. What is Mrs. Johnson doing?

❏ 3. What is the paper boy doing?

❏ 4. What is Happy doing on the lawn?

❏ 5. What is Happy doing "happily" in the corner?

Homework: Take a copy of this story and word/picture list home, and follow the directions above.

_____   _____   _____
Name   Homework Partner   Date

Is Verb+ing

#BK-309 Grammar Tickle Stories™ • ©2004 Super Duper® Publications • 1-800-277-8737 • Online! www.superduperinc.com

Ocean Spray Park

Directions: Give each student a list of the Picture Words on page 80 or the Word List on page 81. Do not reveal the story title. Ask each student for "words" from his/her page to fill in the spaces in the story below. Write the words in the spaces. You may also have the student write these words on his/her Companion Activity Sheet (page 87). Then, have the student read/listen to the story. For more options, see *How To Use This Book* on page ii.

Boys and girls, please direct your attention to the left side of the pool, where

Sharmo _____ and getting ready to entertain you. In the pool on
(is verb+ing)

the right, her brother, Omar, _____. This helps him to warm up.
(is verb+ing)

The trainer _____ her whistle. Here comes Sharmo! Let's give
(is verb+ing)

her a warm round of applause. She _____ so easily. You
(is verb+ing)

wouldn't know that it took her two years to learn to do that trick. Now, her brother Omar

_____. Here comes the grande finale. Sharmo
(is verb+ing)

_____ and Omar _____ at the same
(is verb+ing)   (is verb+ing)

time! Let's give them a big hand as their trainer _____ and
(is verb+ing)

giving them their fish reward.

Have a great rest of the day at *Ocean Spray Park*!

Questions: (Answer in a complete sentence.)

❑ 1. What is Sharmo doing while she is getting ready to entertain you?

❑ 2. What is Omar doing, which helps him warm up?

❑ 3. What is the trainer doing with her whistle?

❑ 4. What is Sharmo doing that took her two years to learn?

❑ 5. What is Sharmo doing and what is Omar doing in the grande finale?

Homework: Take a copy of this story and word/picture list home, and follow the directions above.

_____   _____   _____   **Is Verb+ing**
Name   Homework Partner   Date

The Problem Club

Directions: Give each student a list of the Picture Words on page 80 or the Word List on page 81. Do not reveal the story title. Ask each student for "words" from his/her page to fill in the spaces in the story below. Write the words in the spaces. You may also have the student write these words on his/her Companion Activity Sheet (page 87). Then, have the student read/listen to the story. For more options, see *How To Use This Book* on page ii.

_____ your problem? Welcome to the *Problem Club*.
(is verb+ing)

We can help you with any problem that you can't handle. Let's watch this video and

you'll see what I mean. This first lady _____. She was
(is verb+ing)

not able to solve this problem until she came to the *Problem Club*. Now, she

_____ and is much happier. Watch this boy. He
(is verb+ing)

_____ and couldn't stop until he came to us for help. Now
(is verb+ing)

he _____ in a whole new way. If your sister
(is verb+ing)

_____, or your brother _____, or
(is verb+ing)   (is verb+ing)

anyone you know _____, have them call 555-PROBLEM.
(is verb+ing)

We can solve all of your problems!

Questions: (Answer in a complete sentence.)

❑ 1. What is the lady in the video doing?

❑ 2. What is the lady in the video doing after she came to the Problem Club?

❑ 3. What is the boy in the video doing?

❑ 4. What is the boy doing after coming to the Problem Club?

❑ 5. What does the "announcer" ask about your sister or brother?

Homework: Take a copy of this story and word/picture list home, and follow the directions above.

_____   _____   _____
Name   Homework Partner   Date

Is Verb+ing

#BK-309 Grammar Tickle Stories™ • ©2004 Super Duper® Publications • 1-800-277-8737 • Online! www.superduperinc.com

Present-ing New Nursery Rhymes

Directions: Give each student a list of the Picture Words on page 80 or the Word List on page 81. Do not reveal the story title. Ask each student for "words" from his/her page to fill in the spaces in the story below. Write the words in the spaces. You may also have the student write these words on his/her Companion Activity Sheet (page 87). Then, have the student read/listen to the story. For more options, see *How To Use This Book* on page ii.

Gather around children and listen to Mother Goose as you've never heard before!

Little Boy Blue _____ his horn.
(is verb+ing)
The sheep's in the meadow, the cow's in the corn.

Where is the boy who looks after the sheep?

He _____ in the hayloft and falling asleep!
(is verb+ing)

Hey diddle diddle, the cat and the fiddle,

the cow _____ over the moon!
(is verb+ing)
The dog _____ to see such sport
(is verb+ing)
and the dish _____ with the spoon!
(is verb+ing)

London Bridge _____ down, _____ down,
(is verb+ing) (is verb+ing)
_____ down. London Bridge _____
(is verb+ing) (is verb+ing)
down, my fair lady!

Well children, so how did you like this new Mother Goose?

Questions: (Answer in a complete sentence.)
- ❏ 1. What is Little Boy Blue doing?
- ❏ 2. What is Little Boy Blue doing in the hayloft?
- ❏ 3. What is the cow doing over the moon?
- ❏ 4. What is the dish doing with the spoon?
- ❏ 5. What is London Bridge doing?

Homework: Take a copy of this story and word/picture list home, and follow the directions above.

_____ _____ _____

Name   Homework Partner   Date   **Is Verb+ing**

At the Fair

Directions: Give each student a list of the Picture Words on page 80 or the Word List on page 81. Do not reveal the story title. Ask each student for "words" from his/her page to fill in the spaces in the story below. Write the words in the spaces. You may also have the student write these words on his/her Companion Activity Sheet (page 87). Then, have the student read/listen to the story. For more options, see *How To Use This Book* on page ii.

Reporting From the County Fair: Hoot UhNanny

It's a beautiful day at the County Fair. The sun _____. Over in

(is verb+ing)

the animal section, the judging is going on for the best pig. Little Susie's prize pig

_____, and the judges love it! Johnny Anderson's piglet

(is verb+ing)

_____ and making everyone laugh. It's going to be hard to "pig" a

(is verb+ing)

winner this year, folks. Over at the game section, Bobby Sue _____,

(is verb+ing)

trying to win a prize stuffed porcupine. (Ouch!) Mrs. Summersday _____

(is verb+ing)

because her peach pie took first place again this year! The Big Bandstand is rockin' with the

sounds of Country Cousins. Mayor Fred _____ right alongside them!

(is verb+ing)

Baby Maizy _____ because the music is too loud for her, but everyone

(is verb+ing)

else _____, having a great time! So, come on down and join the fun.

(is verb+ing)

This is Hoot UhNanny reporting from the County Fair.

Questions: (Answer in a complete sentence.)
- ❏ 1. What is the sun doing?
- ❏ 2. What is little Susie's prize pig doing? Johnny Anderson's piglet?
- ❏ 3. What is Bobby Sue doing?
- ❏ 4. What is Mayor Fred doing right alongside the band?
- ❏ 5. What is Baby Maizy doing?

Homework: Take a copy of this story and word/picture list home, and follow the directions above.

_____   _____   _____
Name   Homework Partner   Date

Is Verb+ing

#BK-309 Grammar Tickle Stories™ • ©2004 Super Duper® Publications • 1-800-277-8737 • Online! www.superduperinc.com

Is Verb+ing Companion Activity Sheet

Directions: During or following the story, have the student write words from the word or picture list on the lines below. Then, have the student write sentences with these words in them.

Example: ___ *is reading* ___

*My sister **is reading** her favorite book.*

1. _____

_____

2. _____

_____

3. _____

_____

4. _____

_____

5. _____

_____

6. _____

_____

7. _____

_____

8. _____

_____

Homework: ❏ Take a copy of this sheet home with a word/picture list. Then, follow the directions above.

_____   _____   _____   **Is Verb+ing**
Name   Homework Partner   Date

What Is Going On?

Directions: Match the "is verb+ing" phrase on the left with a picture on the right by drawing a line. Say the is verb+ing in a sentence.

is blowing

is falling down

is wagging

is fixing

is rolling

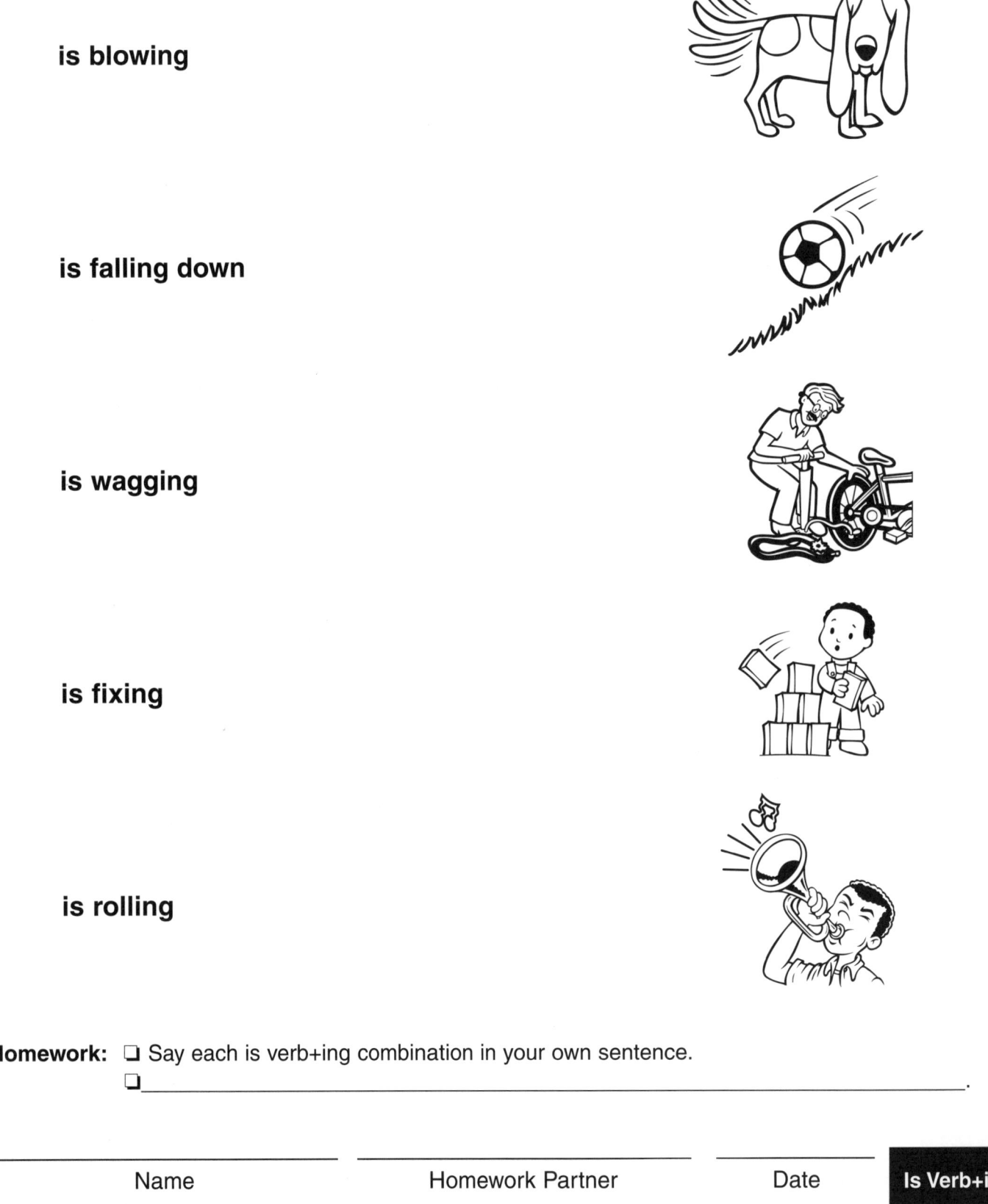

Homework: ❑ Say each is verb+ing combination in your own sentence.

❑ _____.

_____   _____   _____

Name   Homework Partner   Date

Is Verb+ing

#BK-309 Grammar Tickle Stories™ • ©2004 Super Duper® Publications • 1-800-277-8737 • Online! www.superduperinc.com

Activity Card

Is Verb+ing

Tell your homework partner in a complete sentence:

1. Tell what your pet is doing.

2. Find a picture of an animal in a book or magazine and tell what it is doing.

_____   _____
Name   Date

Activity Card

Is Verb+ing

Tell your homework partner in a complete sentence:

1. Tell where your shirt is hanging.

2. Wave your arm in the air and tell what your arm is doing.

_____   _____
Name   Date

Activity Card

Is Verb+ing

Tell your homework partner in a complete sentence:

1. Tell what the clock is doing.

2. Turn on a faucet. Tell what the water is doing.

_____   _____
Name   Date

Activity Card

Is Verb+ing

Tell your homework partner in a complete sentence:

1. Tell what your brother or sister is doing.

2. Tap your finger on the table and tell what your finger is doing.

_____   _____
Name   Date

Is Verb+ing

Is Verb+ing

Tell your homework partner in a complete sentence:

1. Open the door and tell what the door is doing.

2. Look in a book or magazine and tell what one person is doing.

_____
Name

_____
Date

Is Verb+ing

Tell your homework partner in a complete sentence:

1. Turn the light on and tell what the light is doing.

2. Bend your head forward and tell what your head is doing.

_____
Name

_____
Date

Is Verb+ing

Tell your homework partner in a complete sentence:

1. Tell what your favorite stuffed animal is doing.

2. Lick your upper lip with your tongue, then tell what you tongue is doing.

_____
Name

_____
Date

Is Verb+ing

Tell your homework partner in a complete sentence:

1. Close the door and tell what the door is doing.

2. Wink one eye and tell what your eye is doing.

_____
Name

_____
Date

Is Verb+ing

Are Verb+ing

Directions: Use the picture words below to help you complete the stories on pages 93 to 97.

are cleaning

are giggling

are reading

are smelling

are cooking

are hopping

are riding

are smiling

are dancing

are hugging

are running

are swinging

are drawing

are planting

are shopping

are talking

are exercising

are playing

are singing

are watching

are flying

are pulling

are skating

are waving

Are Verb+ing

Are Verb+ing

Directions: Use these words to help complete the stories on pages 93 to 97 and 102 to 106..

❏ are acting
❏ are asking
❏ are baking
❏ are barking
❏ are breaking
❏ are brushing
❏ are buying
❏ are calling
❏ are carrying
❏ are catching
❏ are chasing
❏ are clapping
❏ are cleaning
❏ are climbing
❏ are combing
❏ are cooking
❏ are counting
❏ are crawling
❏ are crying
❏ are cutting
❏ are dancing
❏ are daydreaming
❏ are digging
❏ are drawing
❏ are drinking
❏ are driving
❏ are dusting
❏ are eating
❏ are exercising
❏ are falling
❏ are fishing
❏ are fixing
❏ are flying
❏ are folding
❏ are giggling

❏ are giving
❏ are growling
❏ are helping
❏ are hiding
❏ are hiking
❏ are holding
❏ are hopping
❏ are hugging
❏ are jumping
❏ are keeping
❏ are kissing
❏ are laughing
❏ are leaving
❏ are listening
❏ are looking
❏ are mailing
❏ are mopping
❏ are mowing
❏ are opening
❏ are painting
❏ are pasting
❏ are petting
❏ are planting
❏ are playing
❏ are pouring
❏ are pulling
❏ are racing
❏ are raining
❏ are raking
❏ are reading
❏ are resting
❏ are riding
❏ are ringing
❏ are running
❏ are sailing

❏ are sewing
❏ are shopping
❏ are singing
❏ are sitting
❏ are skating
❏ are skiing
❏ are sleeping
❏ are sliding
❏ are smelling
❏ are smiling
❏ are sneezing
❏ are speaking
❏ are spilling
❏ are splashing
❏ are standing
❏ are studying
❏ are swimming
❏ are swinging
❏ are talking
❏ are thinking
❏ are throwing
❏ are tearing
❏ are teaching
❏ are thanking
❏ are tickling
❏ are walking
❏ are watching
❏ are waving
❏ are wearing
❏ are whistling
❏ are wishing
❏ are writing
❏ are yelling

Are Verb+ing

#BK-309 Grammar Tickle Stories™ • ©2004 Super Duper® Publications • 1-800-277-8737 • Online! www.superduperinc.com

Zoo-Keeny

Directions: Give each student a list of the Picture Words on page 91 or the Word List on page 92. Do not reveal the story title. Ask each student for "words" from his/her page to fill in the spaces in the story below. Write the words in the spaces. You may also have the student write these words on his/her Companion Activity Sheet (page 98). Then, have the student read/listen to the story. For more options, see *How To Use This Book* on page ii.

Grandpa took Sis and Bud to the zoo. First they went to the monkey cage. "Oh look,

the monkeys _____," said Grandpa. Sis and Bud threw them a
                    (are verb+ing)

piece of banana. "Oh look, now they _____ the banana!" Sis said
                                        (are verb+ing)

excitedly. Bud wanted to see the wild animals. "If you hurry," said the Zookeeper, "the

tigers _____ right now!" They ran to the tiger cage. "Look, they
            (are verb+ing)

_____, too!" said Bud. They visited the elephants. "If you walk
        (are verb+ing)

quietly, you can see that those two large elephants _____ by the
                                                        (are verb+ing)

lake," said Grandpa! "Oh, and the babies _____, too," said Sis.
                                            (are verb+ing)

An announcement came over the loudspeaker: "Attention, if you go to the Lion's den,

the Zookeepers _____ the lions right now!" This is something
                (are verb+ing) (with)

Grandpa had always wanted to see! At the end of the day, Grandpa was very tired.

Questions: (Answer in a complete sentence.)
- ❏ 1. What are the monkeys doing?
- ❏ 2. What are the tigers doing?
- ❏ 3. What are the baby elephants doing?
- ❏ 4. What are the zookeepers doing with the lions?
- ❏ 5. How did Grandpa feel at the end of the day?

Homework: Take a copy of this story and word/picture list home, and follow the directions above.

_____   _____   _____ | **Are Verb+ing** |
Name   Homework Partner   Date

Nature Hike

Directions: Give each student a list of the Picture Words on page 91 or the Word List on page 92. Do not reveal the story title. Ask each student for "words" from his/her page to fill in the spaces in the story below. Write the words in the spaces. You may also have the student write these words on his/her Companion Activity Sheet (page 98). Then, have the student read/listen to the story. For more options, see *How To Use This Book* on page ii.

Good morning, campers! I see some of you _____,
(are verb+ing)

getting ready for our long hike today. Let's go over a few rules first. Make sure that

as we _____, you keep your eyes and ears open. If you see a
(are verb+ing)

funny green plant that looks like this, it might be that we _____
(are verb+ing)

too close! If you hear a sound like "Doo - whap," it might be that we

_____ near the endangered Doo Wop Bird. As we climb higher, if
(are verb+ing)

you start to feel dizzy, it could be that you _____, which is a
(are verb+ing)

natural reaction at some heights. Just stop, take three deep breaths, and say to yourself,

"We _____," over and over until you calm down. The hike leaders
(are verb+ing)

_____ now, so let's say our camp cheer, "We
(are verb+ing)

_____," and get ready to hike!
(are verb+ing)

Questions: (Answer in a complete sentence.)

❏ 1. What are we doing when we need to keep our eyes and ears open?

❏ 2. If we hear a "Doo-whap" sound, what are we doing?

❏ 3. If you feel dizzy, what are you doing?

❏ 4. What should you say we are doing after you take three deep breaths?

❏ 5. What is our camp cheer?

Homework: Take a copy of this story and word/picture list home, and follow the directions above.

_____ _____ _____

| Name | Homework Partner | Date | **Are Verb+ing** |

The Spelling Bee

Directions: Give each student a list of the Picture Words on page 91 or the Word List on page 92. Do not reveal the story title. Ask each student for "words" from his/her page to fill in the spaces in the story below. Write the words in the spaces. You may also have the student write these words on his/her Companion Activity Sheet (page 98). Then, have the student read/listen to the story. For more options, see *How To Use This Book* on page ii.

ANNOUNCEMENT

Students, this is to let you know that we are now accepting applications for *The*

Spelling Bee. Your principal, Mrs. Huncklesdorf, is excited to tell you that this year

we _____ and might go to the state finals. If you think this is
(are verb+ing)

something you might like to do as a class, tell yourselves we _____.
(are verb+ing)

It's not that hard to do. Every day, as students, we _____ and the
(are verb+ing)

teachers _____. This is why we gained the reputation that earned
(are verb+ing)

us a High Achievement Award last year. In her acceptance speech, Mrs. Huncklesdorf

said that as a school, we _____ and this year we
(are verb+ing)

_____ to maintain this high standard again. Remember our school
(are verb+ing)

motto: *We* _____ *one and all*. Now, if you can spell Mrs.
(are verb+ing)

Huncklesdorf, then we most certainly _____! Good Luck!
(are verb+ing)

Questions: (Answer in a complete sentence.)
- ❏ 1. What is Mrs. Huncklesdorf excited to tell us that we are doing?
- ❏ 2. What should our class tell ourselves?
- ❏ 3. What are we doing everyday as students? as teachers?
- ❏ 4. What did Mrs. Huncklesdorf say, that as a school, we are doing?
- ❏ 5. What is our school motto?

Homework: Take a copy of this story and word/picture list home, and follow the directions above.

_____   _____   _____   **Are Verb+ing**
Name   Homework Partner   Date

What's Cooking, Class?

Directions: Give each student a list of the Picture Words on page 91 or the Word List on page 92. Do not reveal the story title. Ask each student for "words" from his/her page to fill in the spaces in the story below. Write the words in the spaces. You may also have the student write these words in his/her Companion Activity Sheet (page 98). Then, have the student read/listen to the story. For more options, see *How To Use This Book* on page ii.

Good morning class! Today you'll learn how to be great cooks from some of the world's

greatest chefs! As we _____, we will watch this video. Since
                              (are verb+ing)

you'll be working in pairs, we're going to watch a video of famous chef pairs. First, Chef

Maurice from France and Chef Gino from Italy are teaching us. See how they

_____ the dough? Next, you'll see they _____
        (are verb+ing)   (are verb+ing)

the pan before they put the bread in it. Finally, you'll see that they _____.
                                                                              (are verb+ing)

It is wonderful when you work with a partner. Next, Chef Katrina from the United States and

Chef Arturo from Spain _____ before they ever get ready to cook!
                              (are verb+ing)

Then, they _____ the vegetables to put in the pan. So, now it's time
                  (are verb+ing)

to go to your kitchens. While you _____ with your partner, say to
                                          (are verb+ing)

each other, "We _____." It will help make the food taste even better!
                      (are verb+ing)

Questions: (Answer in a complete sentence.)

❏ 1. What are Chef Maurice and Chef Gino doing to the dough?

❏ 2. What are Chefs Maurice and Gino doing last?

❏ 3. What are Chefs Katrina and Arturo doing before getting ready to cook?

❏ 4. What are Chefs Katrina and Arturo doing to the vegetables?

❏ 5. What are you and your partner supposed to say while you're working?

Homework: Take a copy of this story and word/picture list home, and follow the directions above.

_____   _____   _____   **Are Verb+ing**
          Name   Homework Partner   Date

How To Get A Good Night's Sleep

Directions: Give each student a list of the Picture Words on page 91 or the Word List on page 92. Do not reveal the story title. Ask each student for "words" from his/her page to fill in the spaces in the story below. Write the words in the spaces. You may also have the student write these words on his/her Companion Activity Sheet (page 98). Then, have the student read/listen to the story. For more options, see *How To Use This Book* on page ii.

If your eyes _____ and your ears _____,
                      (are verb+ing)   (are verb+ing)

then you might not be getting a good night's sleep. We may have just the thing for you,

with our new video *Sleep While You Sleep*. If you put on our soothing video, you'll see

that instead of jumping over a fence, the sheep _____ and
                                       (are verb+ing)

the birds _____ above them. The trees are swaying and
              (are verb+ing)

_____ silently. Soon, you'll notice that you are not hearing any
 (are verb+ing)

sounds and your eyes _____ slowly. Let your dreams take over.
                          (are verb+ing)

You might dream that ships _____ on the ocean, or that you
                               (are verb+ing)

_____ quietly on the beach. When you are lulled into a peaceful
  (are verb+ing)

sleep, you'll know that our video, *Sleep While You Sleep,* was just right for you! Sweet

dreams, everyone.

Questions: (Answer in a complete sentence.)

❏ 1. What are your eyes doing if you aren't getting sleep?
❏ 2. What are the sheep in the video doing?
❏ 3. What are the birds in the video doing?
❏ 4. What are the trees in the video doing?
❏ 5. What are the ships doing in the ocean?

Homework: Take a copy of this story and word/picture list home, and follow the directions above.

_____   _____   _____

      Name   Homework Partner   Date

Are Verb+ing

Are Verb+ing Companion Activity Sheet

Directions: During or following the story, have the student write words from the word or picture list on the lines below. Then, have the student write sentences with these words in them.

Example: *are flying*

----

*The children **are flying** colorful kites*

1. _____

_____

2. _____

_____

3. _____

_____

4. _____

_____

5. _____

_____

6. _____

_____

7. _____

_____

8. _____

_____

Homework: ❑ Take a copy of this sheet home with a word/picture list. Then, follow the directions above.

_____ _____ _____ | Are Verb+ing |

Name　　　　　　　　Homework Partner　　　　　　Date

Monkey See, Monkeys Are Doing

Directions: Write the letters **a** through **f** on small cards. Have students roll a die and read the sentence that corresonds to the number on the die. Then, have the student choose a letter card and read the corresponding answer. Enjoy the silly sentences! If a correct match is made, score a point!

1. The monkeys...

2. The elephants...

3. The bird watchers...

4. The chefs...

5. The sheep...

6. The students...

a. ...are eating bananas.

b. ...are drinking water.

c. ...are watching birds.

d. ...are baking cakes.

e. ...are jumping over a fence.

f. ...are spelling words.

Homework: ❏ Say each are verb+ing combination in your own sentence. Draw a picture of your favorite silly combination. Bring it back for your group to see.

❏ _____.

| Name | Homework Partner | Date |

Are Verb+ing

Are Verb+ing

Tell your homework partner in a complete sentence:

1. Tell where the cars are parking.

2. Flap your bent arms like a chicken and tell what your arms are doing.

_____ _____
Name   Date

Are Verb+ing

Tell your homework partner in a complete sentence:

1. Tell where the books are sitting.

2. Find a picture of people in a book or a magazine and tell what they are doing.

_____ _____
Name   Date

Are Verb+ing

Tell your homework partner in a complete sentence:

1. Tell where your shoes are sitting.

2. Wiggle your toes and tell what they are doing.

_____ _____
Name   Date

Are Verb+ing

Tell your homework partner in a complete sentence:

1. Tell where the flowers are growing.

2. Blink your eyes and tell what your eyes are doing.

_____ _____
Name   Date

Are Verb+ing

#BK-309 Grammar Tickle Stories™ • ©2004 Super Duper® Publications • 1-800-277-8737 • Online! www.superduperinc.com

Are Verb+ing

Tell your homework partner in a complete sentence:

1. Tell where your toys are sitting.

2. Clap your hands and tell what your hands are doing.

_____ _____
Name   Date

Are Verb+ing

Tell your homework partner in a complete sentence:

1. Tell where the clothes are drying.

2. Look in the closet and tell where your clothes are hanging.

_____ _____
Name   Date

Are Verb+ing

Tell your homework partner in a complete sentence:

1. Tell where the clothes are washing.

2. Snap your fingers and tell what your fingers are doing.

_____ _____
Name   Date

Are Verb+ing

Tell your homework partner in a complete sentence:

1. Open the freezer and tell where the ice cubes are freezing.

2. Put some ice cubes in a glass and listen to them clink. Then, tell what the ice cubes are doing.

_____ _____
Name   Date

Are Verb+ing

Uncle Joe's Trained Birds

Directions: Give each student a list of the Picture Words on pages 80 and 91 or the Word Lists on pages 81 and 92. Do not reveal the story title. Ask each student for "words" from his/her page to fill in the spaces in the story below. Write the words in the spaces. You may also have the student write these words on his/her Companion Activity Sheet (page 107). Then, have the student read/listen to the story. For more options, see *How To Use This Book* on page ii.

Mary and John's uncle, Joe, trains birds. Today, Uncle Joe invited them over to

see him work. "I love it when Uncle Joe _____," says Mary, "I
(is verb+ing)

could watch him for hours!" "Especially when his birds _____,"
(are verb+ing)

added John.   Uncle Joe said he would teach Mary and John some bird tricks. First,

he showed Mary. "Look," Uncle Joe said to John, "Mary _____
(is verb+ing)

and she learned quickly! The parrots _____ because they
(are verb+ing)

see her signal!" "Let me try," said John. "Look," Uncle Joe said to Mary, "John

_____ and the doves _____! But that small
(is verb+ing)   (are verb+ing)

bird in the corner _____ all by herself." "I wonder," said
(is verb+ing)

Uncle Joe, "if the birds watch us and say, 'We love to watch Mary, John and Uncle Joe

when they _____'." Then, the birds started to chirp. Everyone
(are verb+ing)

laughed together!

Questions: (Answer in a complete sentence.)

❏ 1. Mary loves to watch Uncle Joe. What is he doing?

❏ 2. What is Mary doing that she is learning quickly?

❏ 3. When Mary is doing that, what are the parrots doing?

❏ 4. What is John doing and what are the doves doing?

❏ 5. What does Uncle Joe imagine the birds are saying about Mary, John and Uncle Joe?

Homework: Take a copy of this story and word/picture list home, and follow the directions above.

_____   _____   _____

Name   Homework Partner   Date

Is/Are Verb+ing Combo

#BK-309 Grammar Tickle Stories™ • ©2004 Super Duper® Publications • 1-800-277-8737 • Online! www.superduperinc.com

Computer Class

Directions: Give each student a list of the Picture Words on pages 80 and 91 or the Word Lists on pages 81 and 92. Do not reveal the story title. Ask each student for "words" from his/her page to fill in the spaces in the story below. Write the words in the spaces. You may also have the student write these words on his/her Companion Activity Sheet (page 107). Then, have the student read/listen to the story. For more options, see *How To Use This Book* on page ii.

This is a description from a School Class Catalog.

The computer class is now taking sign-ups for the spring course. This class

_____ fast! It's very popular. The students who want to apply for
(is verb+ing)

college _____. Today, more than ever, it is important that each
(are verb+ing)

person _____. Many students sign up for this class with a friend.
(is verb+ing)

That way, you _____ together! Maybe your best friend
(are verb+ing)

_____. Perhaps your parents _____. Don't
(is verb+ing)   (are verb+ing)

be left behind. Last year one parent said this about her daughter. "After taking this

class, my daughter _____ and she could never do that before!"
(is verb+ing)

Our instructor said this about his students last year. "I have students who

_____ on their own. They are so anxious to learn." If you are
(are verb+ing)

interested in taking this class, please fill out the form below and drop it by the main office.

Questions: (Answer in a complete sentence.)

❏ 1. What are students doing who want to apply for college?

❏ 2. Today, it is more important than ever that each person is doing what?

❏ 3. If you sign up for a class, then you are doing what together?

❏ 4. What is one student doing according to her parent, that she couldn't do before?

❏ 5. What are eager students doing on their own?

Homework: Take a copy of this story and word/picture list home, and follow the directions above.

_____   _____   _____   **Is/Are Verb+ing**
Name   Homework Partner   Date   **Combo**

Shoes On The Run

Directions: Give each student a list of the Picture Words on pages 80 and 91 or the Word Lists on pages 81 and 92. Do not reveal the story title. Ask each student for "words" from his/her page to fill in the spaces in the story below. Write the words in the spaces. You may also have the student write these words on his/her Companion Activity Sheet (page 107). Then, have the student read/listen to the story. For more options, see *How To Use This Book* on page ii.

This is an advertisement for new running shoes.

"Oh no, my shoes _____. My left shoe _____,
(are verb+ing)   (is verb+ing)

while my right shoe _____." Does this sound familiar to you? If
(is verb+ing)

you looked at your shoes this morning and said, "With these shoes on, my feet

_____," then this ad is for you. These are the new *Fast and Furious*
(are verb+ing)

Feet running shoes by *Gogetum*. These shoes _____ just when you
(are verb+ing)

need them to! You may think that this claim _____ your leg. That's
(is verb+ing)

kind of funny, in fact, because they _____ your feet! But, these shoes
(are verb+ing)

are built to last! The *Gogetum* company _____ solidly behind their
(is verb+ing)

claims. You will be the fastest runner on your block!

Questions: (Answer in a complete sentence.)

❏ 1. The ad asks if you ever say, "Oh no, my shoes"...what?

❏ 2. What is my left shoe doing?

❏ 3. What is my right shoe doing?

❏ 4. What are these new shoes doing just when you need them to?

❏ 5. What is the company doing solidly behind the claims of these shoes?

Homework: Take a copy of this story and word/picture list home, and follow the directions above.

_____   _____   _____   **Is/Are Verb+ing**
            Name   Homework Partner   Date   **Combo**

#BK-309 Grammar Tickle Stories™ • ©2004 Super Duper® Publications • 1-800-277-8737 • Online! www.superduperinc.com

The Plot Thickens

Directions: Give each student a list of the Picture Words on pages 80 and 91 or the Word Lists on pages 81 and 92. Do not reveal the story title. Ask each student for "words" from his/her page to fill in the spaces in the story below. Write the words in the spaces. You may also have the student write these words on his/her Companion Activity Sheet (page 107). Then, have the student read/listen to the story. For more options, see *How To Use This Book* on page ii.

The following is a pilot (trial) for a new TV show.

Pete and Katie live in this small neighborhood with their mom, dad, and two Golden

Retrievers, Dudley and Donut. As the scene opens, the children _____.

(are verb+ing)

Suddenly, without warning, they hear a noise behind them. Donut _____

(is verb+ing)

loudly. "What could that be?" asks Pete. "Let's go find Mom and Dad," says Katie.

Meanwhile, Mom and Dad _____ in the backyard, getting ready for

(are verb+ing)

spring. "Mom, Dad!" Pete says, "Dudley _____. What could it be?"

(is verb+ing)

"Oh, I was afraid this would happen some day," says Mom. She tells Pete and Katie about

an old family secret. The audience, (that's us), _____ anxiously to

(is verb+ing)

know the secret. Unfortunately, Donut _____ suddenly. We know

(is verb+ing)

we'll have to wait until next week to find out. The previews for the next show reveal that,

while Dad _____, the kids _____.

(is verb+ing)   (are verb+ing)

Tune in next time and see what happens!

Questions: (Answer in a complete sentence.)

- ❏ 1. What are the children doing as the scene opens?
- ❏ 2. What is Donut doing?
- ❏ 3. What are Mom and Dad doing in the backyard?
- ❏ 4. What is Dudley doing?
- ❏ 5. What is Dad doing and what are the kids doing in next week's preview?

Homework: Take a copy of this story and word/picture list home, and follow the directions above.

_____   _____   _____
Name   Homework Partner   Date

Is/Are Verb+ing Combo

The Three Little Pigs Minus The Big Bad Wolf

Directions: Give each student a list of the Picture Words on pages 80 and 91 or the Word Lists on pages 81 and 92. Do not reveal the story title. Ask each student for "words" from his/her page to fill in the spaces in the story below. Write the words in the spaces. You may also have the student write these words on his/her Companion Activity Sheet (page 107). Then, have the student read/listen to the story. For more options, see *How To Use This Book* on page ii.

What happens to the Three Little Pigs after the Big Bad Wolf runs away? Let's find

out. The first Little Pig _____ in his house of straw. The second
                        (is verb+ing)

Little Pig, in the stick house, _____ . No wait, he's going to talk to
                                (is verb+ing)

his brother, the third Little Pig, who _____ outside of his brick house.
                                       (is verb+ing)

Now, they _____ together. Later, the second and third Little Pig go
          (are verb+ing)

to get their brother. All three _____ happily outside.
                                (are verb+ing)

"Excuse me, Little Pigs, I don't mean to interrupt while you _____.
                                                            (are verb+ing)

But, how is life since the Big Bad Wolf left the area?" "Well," said the third Little Pig, "just

ask our mother who _____ over there in the yard." "OK, Mrs. Little
                   (is verb+ing)

Pigs, how are things since the Big Bad Wolf left?" "For the first time in ten years we

_____ unafraid!" said Mrs. Little Pigs. "No Wolf, no problem."
(are verb+ing)

Questions: (Answer in a complete sentence.)

- ❏ 1. What is the first little pig doing?
- ❏ 2. What is the third little pig doing outside of his brick house?
- ❏ 3. What are all three little pigs doing when they get together?
- ❏ 4. What is Mrs. Little Pigs doing in the yard?
- ❏ 5. What does Mrs. Little Pigs say they are doing for the first time in ten years?

Homework: Take a copy of this story and word/picture list home, and follow the directions above.

			Is/Are Verb+ing
Name	Homework Partner	Date	Combo

#BK-309 Grammar Tickle Stories™ • ©2004 Super Duper® Publications • 1-800-277-8737 • Online! www.superduperinc.com

Is/Are Verb+ing Combo Companion Activity Sheet

Directions: During or following the story, have the student write words from the word or picture list on the lines below. Then, have the student write sentences with these words in them.

Example: _____***is reading***_____ - OR - _____***are flying***_____

My sister **is reading** her favorite book. _The children **are flying** colorful kites._

1. _____

_____

2. _____

_____

3. _____

_____

4. _____

_____

5. _____

_____

6. _____

_____

7. _____

_____

8. _____

_____

Homework: ❑ Take a copy of this sheet home with a word/picture list. Then, follow the directions above.

_____ _____ _____
Name Homework Partner Date

Is/Are Verb+ing Combo

The Mystery/Mysteries Is/Are Solved!

Directions: Help solve the is/are mystery. Read the sentence and circle the correct is/are word to complete it.

Uncle Joe's trained birds **is** **are** doing tricks.

A student **is** **are** working on the computer.

Mom and Dad **is** **are** planting a garden.

The new running shoes **is** **are** selling fast!

Donut, the dog, **is** **are** wagging his tail.

The Big Bad Wolf **is** **are** huffing and puffing.

The Three Little Pigs **is** **are** building their houses.

The doves **is** **are** cooing.

Homework: ❑ Complete or share this with your homework partner using the correct is/are verb+ing form in your answer. Say each is/are verb+ing combination in your own sentence.

❑ _____.

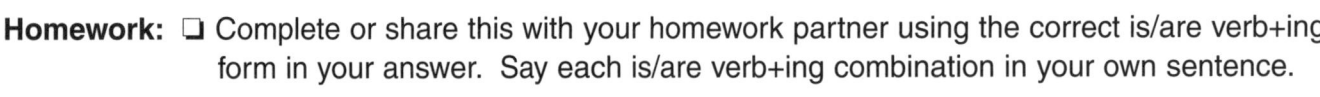

Name	Homework Partner	Date	**Is/Are Verb+ing Combo**

#BK-309 Grammar Tickle Stories™ • ©2004 Super Duper® Publications • 1-800-277-8737 • Online! www.superduperinc.com

Is/Are Verb+ing

Tell your homework partner in a complete sentence:

1. Tell where your bath toys are waiting.

2. Crumple up a piece of paper and tell what the paper is doing.

Name _____

Date _____

Is/Are Verb+ing

Tell your homework partner in a complete sentence:

Look in the sky:

1. Tell if the sun is shining.

2. Tell if the stars are shining.

Name _____

Date _____

Is/Are Verb+ing

Tell your homework partner in a complete sentence:

1. Tell where your backpack is sitting.

2. Tell where the backpacks are hanging when they're at school.

Name _____

Date _____

Is/Are Verb+ing

Tell your homework partner in a complete sentence:

1. Tell what your mom, dad or homework helper is doing.

2. Wiggle your toes. Tell what your toes are doing.

Name _____

Date _____

Is/Are Verb+ing Combo

Is/Are Verb+ing

Find three pictures in a book or magazine that show a person (or thing) doing something and tell what that person (or thing) is doing.

1. The _____ is _____ing.

2. The _____ is _____ing.

3. The _____ is _____ing.

_____ _____
Name   Date

Is/Are Verb+ing

Find three pictures in a book or magazine that show more than one person (or thing) doing something and tell what each person (or thing) is doing.

1. The _____ is _____ing.

2. The _____ is _____ing.

3. The _____ is _____ing.

_____ _____
Name   Date

Is/Are Verb+ing

Answer in a complete sentence using the correct is/are verb+ing form.

1. Are your clothes hanging in the closet?

2. Is your blanket lying on your bed?

_____ _____
Name   Date

Is/Are Verb+ing

Answer in a complete sentence using the correct is/are verb+ing form.

Look Outside!

1. Are children riding bikes on the sidewalk?

2. Is a bird singing in the tree?

_____ _____
Name   Date

Is/Are Verb+ing
Combo

Was and Were
Verb+ing

Was Verb+ing

Directions: Use the picture words below to help you complete the stories on pages 114 to 118 and 134 to 138.

was baking

was crawling

was eating

was reading

was barking

was crying

was fishing

was sewing

was brushing

was cutting

was jumping

was sleeping

was building

was digging

was kicking

was swimming

was clapping

was drinking

was laughing

was throwing

was climbing

was driving

was painting

was writing

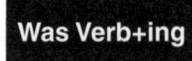

Was Verb+ing

#BK-309 Grammar Tickle Stories™ • ©2004 Super Duper® Publications • 1-800-277-8737 • Online! www.superduperinc.com

Was Verb+ing

Directions: Use these words to help complete the stories on pages 114 to 118 and 134 to 138.

❑ was acting	❑ was helping	
❑ was asking	❑ was hiding	
❑ was baking	❑ was hiking	
❑ was barking	❑ was holding	
❑ was breaking	❑ was hopping	
❑ was brushing	❑ was hugging	❑ was skating
❑ was buying	❑ was jumping	❑ was skiing
❑ was climbing	❑ was keeping	❑ was sleeping
❑ was cooking	❑ was kissing	❑ was sliding
❑ was crying	❑ was leaving	❑ was smelling
❑ was calling	❑ was listening	❑ was smiling
❑ was carrying	❑ was looking	❑ was sneezing
❑ was catching	❑ was laughing	❑ was speaking
❑ was chasing	❑ was mowing	❑ was spilling
❑ was clapping	❑ was mopping	❑ was spinning
❑ was cleaning	❑ was mailing	❑ was splashing
❑ was combing	❑ was opening	❑ was standing
❑ was counting	❑ was painting	❑ was studying
❑ was crawling	❑ was pasting	❑ was swimming
❑ was cutting	❑ was petting	❑ was swinging
❑ was driving	❑ was planting	❑ was talking
❑ was dancing	❑ was playing	❑ was thinking
❑ was daydreaming	❑ was pouring	❑ was throwing
❑ was digging	❑ was pulling	❑ was tearing
❑ was drawing	❑ was racing	❑ was teaching
❑ was drinking	❑ was raining	❑ was thanking
❑ was dusting	❑ was raking	❑ was tickling
❑ was eating	❑ was reading	❑ was walking
❑ was exercising	❑ was resting	❑ was watching
❑ was falling	❑ was riding	❑ was waving
❑ was fishing	❑ was ringing	❑ was wearing
❑ was fixing	❑ was running	❑ was whistling
❑ was flying	❑ was sailing	❑ was wishing
❑ was folding	❑ was sewing	❑ was working
❑ was giggling	❑ was shopping	❑ was writing
❑ was giving	❑ was singing	❑ was yelling
❑ was growing	❑ was sitting	

Was Verb+ing

An Old Timer's Story

Directions: Give each student a list of the Picture Words on page 112 or the Word List on page 113. Do not reveal the story title. Ask the student for "words" from his/her page to fill in the spaces in the story below. Write the words in the spaces. You may also have the student write these words on his/her Companion Activity Sheet (page 119). Then, have the student read/listen to the story. For more options, see *How To Use This Book* on page ii.

Grandpa gathered us around the campfire to tell us about when he was a boy in the

woods of Tennessee. He'd say, "Why, when I was a boy, I _____

(was verb+ing)

by the time I was five." He'd slap his knee and say, "I _____ before

(was verb+ing)

I learned how to walk." My eyes widened. I _____ just hearing it!

(was verb+ing)

"That sounds hard Grandpa," I said. He laughed, "Sonny, I _____

(was verb+ing)

with my sisters and brothers from the time we woke up till the time we went to sleep.

When I wasn't doing that, I _____ in the fields. I also

(was verb+ing)

_____ in the barn. It was just expected of us kids." Well, by now

(was verb+ing)

I _____. But then, I thought about it. One day, I'll probably be

(was verb+ing)

sitting around the campfire, talking to my grandchildren, and I'll be saying, "Why, when I

was a boy, I _____ by the time I was five!" Wouldn't my

(was verb+ing)

grandchildren be surprised at that!

Questions: (Answer in a complete sentence.)

- ❏ 1. How did Grandpa start out his story?
- ❏ 2. Tell what Grandpa said he was doing with his brothers and sisters.
- ❏ 3. Tell what Grandpa said he was doing in the fields.
- ❏ 4. Tell what Grandpa said he was doing in the barn.
- ❏ 5. Tell what the boy in the story thought he'd say to his own grandkids some day.

Homework: Take a copy of this story and word/picture list home, and follow the directions above.

_____   _____   _____
Name   Homework Partner   Date   **Was Verb+ing**

#BK-309 Grammar Tickle Stories™ • ©2004 Super Duper® Publications • 1-800-277-8737 • Online! www.superduperinc.com

The Argument

Directions: Give each student a list of the Picture Words on page 112 or the Word List on page 113. Do not reveal the story title. Ask the student for "words" from his/her page to fill in the spaces in the story below. Write the words in the spaces. You may also have the student write these words on his/her Companion Activity Sheet (page119). Then, have the student read/listen to the story. For more options, see *How To Use This Book* on page ii.

Mom came running into the room. "I _____ when I heard this

(was verb+ing)

awful noise," she said to the twins, Bonnie and Johnny. "It was his fault," said Bonnie.

"I _____ all by myself and then he started bothering me." "I

(was verb+ing)

_____," said Johnny, " when she came in and started bothering

(was verb+ing)

me." They both started to get red faces. Just then, Dad came in. "I

_____ in the garage when I heard all this noise," said Dad.

(was verb+ing)

"What's going on?" "Bonnie says Johnny _____ and Johnny

(was verb+ing)

says that Bonnie _____," explained Mom. Dad had an idea,

(was verb+ing)

"You know what, I _____ and an idea came to me. If two children

(was verb+ing)

I know can work together and clean up these toys, I might be in the

mood for ice cream." "I _____ that same idea," said Mom. Before

(was verb+ing)

you could say "vanilla" the whole place was clean!

Questions: (Answer in a complete sentence.)
- ❏ 1. What was Mom doing when she heard the noise?
- ❏ 2. What did Johnny say he was doing?
- ❏ 3. What did Bonnie say she was doing?
- ❏ 4. What did Dad say he was doing in the garage?
- ❏ 5. What did Dad say he was doing when an idea came to him?

Homework: Take a copy of this story and word/picture list home, and follow the directions above.

| Name | Homework Partner | Date | **Was Verb+ing** |

As Told By The Spider

Directions: Give each student a list of the Picture Words on page 112 or the Word List on page 113. Do not reveal the story title. Ask the student for "words" from his/her page to fill in the spaces in the story below. Write the words in the spaces. You may also have the student write these words on his/her Companion Activity Sheet (page 119). Then, have the student read/listen to the story. For more options, see *How To Use This Book* on page ii.

Okay, here's how it really happened. I _____, when I heard
(was verb+ing)

a noise. This little girl came down the road. She _____. My
(was verb+ing)

friend, the beetle, _____ next to me and will tell you the same
(was verb+ing)

thing. So, this little girl stopped and sat on this tuffet. She _____
(was verb+ing)

over and over. Then, she looked up and saw me. I _____ very
(was verb+ing)

quietly, and for no reason, she screamed. She _____ like she
(was verb+ing)

had seen a ghost. I sat down beside her and tried to calm her down. "Little girl,"

I said, "I _____ and didn't mean you any harm." Well, the little
(was verb+ing)

girl jumped up and as she _____, her curds and whey spilled
(was verb+ing)

all over the ground! I tried to call her back, but she ran away. So, Beetle and I ate

her food all up. And that's the truth!

Questions: (Answer in a complete sentence.)

❑ 1. What was the spider doing when he heard a noise?

❑ 2. What was Beetle doing?

❑ 3. What was the little girl doing over and over when she saw the spider?

❑ 4. What was the spider doing quietly?

❑ 5. What was the little girl doing that spilled her curds and whey?

Homework: Take a copy of this story and word/picture list home, and follow the directions above.

Name	Homework Partner	Date

Was Verb+ing

#BK-309 Grammar Tickle Stories™ • ©2004 Super Duper® Publications • 1-800-277-8737 • Online! www.superduperinc.com

Jill Tells All

Directions: Give each student a list of the Picture Words on page 112 or the Word List on page 113. Do not reveal the story title. Ask the student for "words" from his/her page to fill in the spaces in the story below. Write the words in the spaces. You may also have the student write these words on his/her Companion Activity Sheet (page 119). Then, have the student read/listen to the story. For more options, see *How To Use This Book* on page ii.

Jack's mother wanted to know how he fell down the hill. This is Jill's story.

"I _____ in my yard when Jack came by and asked if I wanted to
(was verb+ing)

go up the hill. He _____ and had the pail with him. I said, 'Sure.' So,
(was verb+ing)

we started up the hill. I _____ and he thought it was funny. We both
(was verb+ing)

laughed. Then, while he _____ , he tripped over a rock and fell down
(was verb+ing)

the hill. Jack _____ when this happened, so I thought he was okay.
(was verb+ing)

But then, he ran home to bandage his forehead. I _____ and did not
(was verb+ing)

know what to do next. I went to my mom, who_____. She stopped to
(was verb+ing)

talk to me. She said I should come and tell you straight away. Is Jack okay?"

Just then, Jill saw that Jack _____ outside. He was going to be fine.
(was verb+ing)

His mother just smiled.

Questions: (Answer in a complete sentence.)

❏ 1. What was Jill doing in her yard when Jack came by?

❏ 2. What was Jack doing when he had the pail?

❏ 3. What was Jack doing when he tripped?

❏ 4. What was Jill doing when Jack ran home?

❏ 5. What was Jack doing outside that let Jill know he was okay ?

Homework: Take a copy of this story and word/picture list home, and follow the directions above.

_____   _____   _____   **Was Verb+ing**
Name   Homework Partner   Date

Chicken Little A Little Different

Directions: Give each student a list of the Picture Words on page 112 or the Word List on page 113. Do not reveal the story title. Ask the student for "words" from his/her page to fill in the spaces in the story below. Write the words in the spaces. You may also have the student write these words on his/her Companion Activity Sheet (page 119). Then, have the student read/listen to the story. For more options, see *How To Use This Book* on page ii.

Chicken Little _____ when suddenly, an acorn hit her on the
                          (was verb+ing)

head. "The sky is falling. I must go tell the King," she said. Chicken Little ran into

Henny Penny, who _____. Henny Penny joined Chicken Little to go
                          (was verb+ing)

tell the King. Along the road, they met Ducky Lucky, who _____.
                                                                  (was verb+ing)

Soon, the three were on the road to see the King. They met Goosey Loosey who

_____, but she decided to go with them. They ran down the path
        (was verb+ing)

and all of a sudden they saw Foxy Loxy, who _____. He told
                                                      (was verb+ing)

them he knew a shortcut to the King's castle, but he _____.
                                                              (was verb+ing)

They knew not to believe him. They ran away to see the King. That day, the

King _____, but agreed to see them. The Queen
            (was verb+ing)

_____, but she stopped to listen. They were delighted with
        (was verb+ing)

Chicken Little's story and let them all stay for lunch. They all had some acorn soup!

Questions: (Answer in a complete sentence.)

- ❑ 1. What was Chicken Little doing when an acorn fell on her head?
- ❑ 2. What was Henny Penny doing?
- ❑ 3. What was Foxy Loxy doing?
- ❑ 4. What was the King doing?
- ❑ 5. What was the Queen doing before she stopped to listen?

Homework: Take a copy of this story and word/picture list home, and follow the directions above.

_____	_____	_____
Name	Homework Partner	Date

Was Verb+ing

#BK-309 Grammar Tickle Stories™ • ©2004 Super Duper® Publications • 1-800-277-8737 • Online! www.superduperinc.com

Was Verb+ing Companion Activity Sheet

Directions: During or following the story, have the student write words from the word or picture list on the lines below. Then, have the student write sentences with these words in them.

Example: _____ **was barking** _____

Last night, my dog **was barking** very loudly.

1. _____

_____

2. _____

_____

3. _____

_____

4. _____

_____

5. _____

_____

6. _____

_____

7. _____

_____

8. _____

_____

Homework: ❏ Take a copy of this sheet home with a word/picture list. Then, follow the directions above.

_____   _____   _____ | Was Verb+ing |
Name   Homework Partner   Date

What Was That?

Directions: Read the was verb+ing word answers in the word bank. Then, read the sentences below and write the correct answers in the spaces proveded.

1. When he was just five, the "oldtimer" _____ _____ on his parent's farm.

2. Mom _____ _____ a cake, when she heard the noise and came running.

3. Little Miss Muffett _____ _____ loudly, as if she'd seen a ghost!

4. The spider _____ _____ his web with fine silky thread.

5. Jill _____ _____ jump rope when Jack asked her if she wanted to help him get water.

6. Chicken Little _____ _____ an egg when an acorn hit her on the head.

Word Bank	
was yelling	was laying
was playing	was baking
was working	was spinning

Homework: ❑ Say each was verb+ing combination in your own sentence.

❑ _____.

_____   _____   _____
Name   Homework Partner   Date

Was Verb+ing

#BK-309 Grammar Tickle Stories™ • ©2004 Super Duper® Publications • 1-800-277-8737 • Online! www.superduperinc.com

Was Verb+ing

Tell your homework partner in a complete sentence:

1. Tell what the teacher was doing in school today.

2. Tell why the teacher was doing that in school today.

3. Tell when the teacher was doing that today.

_____ _____
Name Date

Was Verb+ing

Tell your homework partner in a complete sentence:

1. Tell what your friend was doing in school today.

2. Tell where your friend was doing that in school today.

3. Tell when your friend was doing that in school today.

_____ _____
Name Date

Was Verb+ing

Tell your homework partner in a complete sentence:

1. Tell what the sun was doing today.

2. Tell why the sun was doing that today.

3. Tell when the sun was doing that today.

_____ _____
Name Date

Was Verb+ing

Tell your homework partner in a complete sentence:

1. Tell what the moon was doing last night.

2. Tell when the moon was doing that last night.

3. Tell where the moon was doing that last night.

_____ _____
Name Date

Was Verb+ing

Was Verb+ing

Tell your homework partner in a complete sentence:

1. Tell what you were doing five minutes ago.

2. Tell where you were doing something five minutes ago.

3. Tell why you were doing that five minutes ago.

Name _____

Date _____

Was Verb+ing

Finish these sentences:

1. Today, my mom was driving _____.

2. Today, my friend was playing _____.

3. Today, I was running _____.

Name _____

Date _____

Was Verb+ing

Tell your homework partner in a complete sentence:

1. Tell what a person on TV was saying.

2. Tell when a person on TV was talking.

3. Tell where a person on TV was saying it.

Name _____

Date _____

Was Verb+ing

Finish these sentences:

1. Today, I was reading _____.

2. Today, I was thinking about _____.

3. Today, I was playing with _____.

Name _____

Date _____

Was Verb+ing

Were Verb+ing

Directions: Use the picture words below to help you complete the stories on pages 125 to 129 and 134 to 138.

were cleaning

were giggling

were reading

were smelling

were cooking

were hopping

were riding

were smiling

were dancing

were hugging

were running

were swinging

were drawing

were planting

were shopping

were talking

were exercising

were playing

were singing

were watching

were flying

were pulling

were skating

were waving

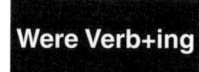

Were Verb+ing

Were Verb+ing

Directions: Use these words to help complete the stories on pages 125 to 129 and 134 to 138.

- ❑ were acting
- ❑ were asking
- ❑ were baking
- ❑ were barking
- ❑ were breaking
- ❑ were brushing
- ❑ were buying
- ❑ were calling
- ❑ were carrying
- ❑ were catching
- ❑ were chasing
- ❑ were clapping
- ❑ were cleaning
- ❑ were climbing
- ❑ were combing
- ❑ were cooking
- ❑ were counting
- ❑ were crawling
- ❑ were crying
- ❑ were cutting
- ❑ were dancing
- ❑ were daydreaming
- ❑ were digging
- ❑ were drawing
- ❑ were drinking
- ❑ were driving
- ❑ were dusting
- ❑ were eating
- ❑ were exercising
- ❑ were falling
- ❑ were fishing
- ❑ were fixing
- ❑ were flying
- ❑ were folding
- ❑ were giggling
- ❑ were giving
- ❑ were growing
- ❑ were helping

- ❑ were hiding
- ❑ were hiking
- ❑ were holding
- ❑ were hopping
- ❑ were hugging
- ❑ were jumping
- ❑ were keeping
- ❑ were kissing
- ❑ were laughing
- ❑ were leaving
- ❑ were listening
- ❑ were looking
- ❑ were mailing
- ❑ were mopping
- ❑ were mowing
- ❑ were opening
- ❑ were painting
- ❑ were pasting
- ❑ were petting
- ❑ were planting
- ❑ were playing
- ❑ were pouring
- ❑ were pulling
- ❑ were racing
- ❑ were raining
- ❑ were raking
- ❑ were resting
- ❑ were riding
- ❑ were ringing
- ❑ were running
- ❑ were sailing
- ❑ were sewing
- ❑ were shopping
- ❑ were singing
- ❑ were sitting
- ❑ were skating
- ❑ were skiing
- ❑ were sleeping

- ❑ were sliding
- ❑ were smelling
- ❑ were smiling
- ❑ were sneezing
- ❑ were speaking
- ❑ were spilling
- ❑ were splashing
- ❑ were standing
- ❑ were studying
- ❑ were swimming
- ❑ were swinging
- ❑ were talking
- ❑ were teaching
- ❑ were tearing
- ❑ were thanking
- ❑ were thinking
- ❑ were throwing
- ❑ were tickling
- ❑ were walking
- ❑ were watching
- ❑ were waving
- ❑ were wearing
- ❑ were whistling
- ❑ were wishing
- ❑ were writing
- ❑ were yelling

Were Verb+ing

#BK-309 Grammar Tickle Stories™ • ©2004 Super Duper® Publications • 1-800-277-8737 • Online! www.superduperinc.com

Letter From Aunt Bee

Directions: Give each student a list of the Picture Words on page 123 or the Word List on page 124. Do not reveal the story title. Ask the student for "words" from his/her page to fill in the spaces in the story below. Write the words in the spaces. You may also have the student write these words on his/her Companion Activity Sheet (page 130). Then, have the student read/listen to the story. For more options, see *How To Use This Book* on page ii.

Hi Everyone,

Greetings from the sunny beaches of Funama Island! Uncle Ben and I almost

didn't make it! When we walked in to the travel agency, the travel agents

_____. They stopped to let us buy our tickets, but as we left,
(were verb+ing)

they _____ again! At the airport, the ticket takers
(were verb+ing)

_____, and we almost missed our plane! The pilots announced
(were verb+ing)

that the men in the control towers _____. While we waited, the flight
(were verb+ing)

attendants _____, and we were anxious to leave. Finally, the plane
(were verb+ing)

took off and Uncle Ben and I _____ at last! When we arrived at
(were verb+ing)

Funama Island, the bus drivers _____ that afternoon! So, we walked
(were verb+ing)

to our hotel with our luggage, and we _____ all the way. But, the
(were verb+ing)

beach was right outside our door! So here we are and have no plans to move for a week.

Love,

Aunt Bee

Questions: (Answer in a complete sentence.)
❑ 1. What did Aunt Bee say the travel agents were doing?
❑ 2. What did the pilot say the men in the control towers were doing?
❑ 3. What did Aunt Bee say the flight attendants were doing?
❑ 4. What did Aunt Bee say the bus drivers were doing?
❑ 5. What did Aunt Bee and Uncle Ben do on the way to the hotel?

Homework: Take a copy of this story and word/picture list home, and follow the directions above.

_____   _____   _____ | **Were Verb+ ing** |
Name   Homework Partner   Date

What Were They Thinking?

Directions: Give each student a list of the Picture Words on page 123 or the Word List on page 124. Do not reveal the story title. Ask the student for "words" from his/her page to fill in the spaces in the story below. Write the words in the spaces. You may also have the student write these words on his/her Companion Activity Sheet (page 130). Then, have the student read/listen to the story. For more options, see *How To Use This Book* on page ii.

From the 10:00 News

Good evening! Mother Goose reporting to you from the hillside where, just moments

ago, something amazing happened. If I hadn't seen it myself, I wouldn't have believed it.

Just as I arrived, a cat and a fiddle _____. They didn't see me as

(were verb+ing)

they _____. Suddenly, a cow appeared, and then, all three

(were verb+ing)

_____ together. The other reporters _____,

(were verb+ing)   (were verb+ing)

when suddenly a dish and a spoon came by. They _____, which

(were verb+ing)

none of us had ever seen before. The dish and the spoon _____

(were verb+ing)

while the dog, cat, and fiddle _____. I looked at the other

(were verb+ing)

reporters, who by this time _____ so hard that we had to stop this

(were verb+ing)

report.

Now back to you, Humpty Dumpty.

Questions: (Answer in a complete sentence.)
- ❏ 1. What were the cat and the fiddle doing when Mother Goose arrived?
- ❏ 2. What were they all doing when the cow appeared?
- ❏ 3. What were the dog, cat, and fiddle doing together?
- ❏ 4. What were the reporters doing when the dish and the spoon came by?
- ❏ 5. What were the reporters doing that made them stop the report?

Homework: Take a copy of this story and word/picture list home, and follow the directions above.

_____   _____   _____   **Were Verb+ing**

Name   Homework Partner   Date

#BK-309 Grammar Tickle Stories™ • ©2004 Super Duper® Publications • 1-800-277-8737 • Online! www.superduperinc.com

Why I Was Late To School And Other Excuses

Directions: Give each student a list of the Picture Words on page 123 or the Word List on page 124. Do not reveal the story title. Ask the student for "words" from his/her page to fill in the spaces in the story below. Write the words in the spaces. You may also have the student write these words on his/her Companion Activity Sheet (page 130). Then, have the student read/listen to the story. For more options, see *How To Use This Book* on page ii.

Here are the eight top excuses that teachers have sent in from students on why they did not get to school on time.

1. My brother and sister _____.
   (were verb+ing)

2. These aliens came down from earth and _____ and took me on their spaceship.
   (were verb+ing)

3. My parents _____ and didn't have time to take me.
   (were verb+ing)

4. My dog and cat _____, and I had to chase them back home!
   (were verb+ing)

5. My coach said that my teammates _____, and I had to join them.
   (were verb+ing)

6. The kids in my carpool _____, and we got lost.
   (were verb+ing)

7. This weekend, all my relatives _____ and stayed over.
   (were verb+ing)

8. My best friend, Howie, and I _____ and I guess I just forgot.
   (were verb+ing)

What's your best excuse?

Questions: (Answer in a complete sentence.)

❏ 1. What were the brother and sister doing in excuse #1?

❏ 2. What were the aliens doing in excuse #2?

❏ 3. What were the parents doing in excuse #3?

❏ 4. What were the kids in the carpool doing in excuse #6?

❏ 5. What were the relatives all doing in excuse #7?

Homework: Take a copy of this story and word/picture list home, and follow the directions above.

_____   _____   _____ | Were Verb+ing |
Name   Homework Partner   Date

The Owl And The Pussycat Back From Sea

Directions: Give each student a list of the Picture Words on page 123 or the Word List on page 124. Do not reveal the story title. Ask the student for "words" from his/her page to fill in the spaces in the story below. Write the words in the spaces. You may also have the student write these words on his/her Companion Activity Sheet (page 130). Then, have the student read/listen to the story. For more options, see *How To Use This Book* on page ii.

News Flash!

The Owl and the Pussycat, who took off for sea in a pea green boat last year, just arrived back in town.

Reporter: "Owl, when we last saw you and Pussycat, you _____."

(were verb+ing)

Owl: "Well, we _____ in our boat, seeing the world!"

(were verb+ing)

Pussycat: "When we weren't sailing, we _____."

(were verb+ing)

Owl: "One night, we _____ and I looked up at the stars."

(were verb+ing)

Pussycat: "Yes, we _____ that night! It was beautiful."

(were verb+ing)

Owl: "We decided to get married, but we didn't have a ring. We _____

(were verb+ing)

when we came to a land where purple trees grow. We met Piggy-wig who had a ring at the

end of his nose. The three of us _____. He sold us the ring. We got

(were verb+ing)

married and while we _____ by the light of the moon, we got an idea."

(were verb+ing)

Pussycat: "So, now we've come back to take tours to see the purple trees!"

Reporter: " Well, that wraps it up for this reporter. I'm off to meet Piggy-wig!"

Questions: (Answer in a complete sentence.)
- ❏ 1. What were the Owl and Pussycat doing the last time the reporter saw them?
- ❏ 2. What were the Owl and Pussycat doing when they weren't sailing?
- ❏ 3. What were the Owl and Pussycat doing the night they saw the stars?
- ❏ 4. What were Owl, Pussycat and Piggy-wig doing?
- ❏ 5. What were Owl and Pussycat doing by the light of the moon?

Homework: Take a copy of this story and word/picture list home, and follow the directions above.

_____ _____ _____ **Were Verb+ing**

Name   Homework Partner   Date

#BK-309 Grammar Tickle Stories™ • ©2004 Super Duper® Publications • 1-800-277-8737 • Online! www.superduperinc.com

Our Trip To The Beach

Directions: Give each student a list of the Picture Words on page 123 or the Word List on page 124. Do not reveal the story title. Ask the student for "words" from his/her page to fill in the spaces in the story below. Write the words in the spaces. You may also have the student write these words on his/her Companion Activity Sheet (page 130). Then, have the student read/listen to the story. For more options, see *How To Use This Book* on page ii.

Last summer, Grandma and Grandpa surprised us and took us to the beach. My brother

and I _____ quietly when they came in. "We _____
　　　　　　　(were verb+ing)　　　　　　　　　　　　　　　　　　　　　　(were verb+ing)

at home," said Grandma. Grandpa said, "Last weekend we _____, and
　　　　　　　　　　　　　　　　　　　　　　　　　　　　　(were verb+ing)

yesterday we _____. Now we need to do something fun!" We piled in the
　　　　　　　(were verb+ing)

car, and we _____ the whole way there! After we built a sandcastle, we
　　　　　　(were verb+ing)

_____ on the beach when Grandma pulled out a picnic basket. It was
　　　(were verb+ing)

very, very funny because as we _____, I was saying to
　　　　　　　　　　　　　　　　　(were verb+ing)

my brother how hungry it was making me. After a good lunch, we had more energy! In fact, we

_____ when Grandma and Grandpa said it was time to go. We didn't
　(were verb+ing)

want to leave, but on the way home, we fell asleep. I guess we were tired after all.

Questions: (Answer in a complete sentence.)

❑　1. What were the brother and sister doing quietly when Grandma and Grandpa came in?

❑　2. What were Grandma and Grandpa doing at home before they came?

❑　3. What did Grandpa say he and Grandma were doing last weekend?

❑　4. What were the brother and sister doing in the car on the way to the beach?

❑　5. What were the brother and sister doing when it was time to go?

Homework: Take a copy of this story and word/picture list home, and follow the directions above.

_____　　_____　　_____
　　　　　Name　　　　　　　　　　　　Homework Partner　　　　　　　　Date　　　　**Were Verb+ing**

Were Verb+ing Companion Activity Sheet

Directions: During or following the story, have the student write words from the word or picture list on the lines below. Then, have the student write sentences with these words in them.

Example: *__were shopping__*

*Yesterday, we **were shopping** all afternoon.*

1. _____

_____

2. _____

_____

3. _____

_____

4. _____

_____

5. _____

_____

6. _____

_____

7. _____

_____

8. _____

_____

Homework: ❏ Take a copy of this sheet home with a word/picture list. Then, follow the directions above.

_____   _____   _____   **Were Verb+ing**
        Name   Homework Partner   Date

#BK-309 Grammar Tickle Stories™ • ©2004 Super Duper® Publications • 1-800-277-8737 • Online! www.superduperinc.com

Oh They Were, Were They?

Directions: Read the were verb+ing answers in the word box. Then, read the sentences below and write the correct answer in the space.

1. We _____ _____ in the car, on the way to the beach.

2. Uncle Ben and Aunt Bee _____ _____ last summer.

3. The Owl and the Pussycat _____ _____ in a pea green boat.

4. Aliens _____ _____ their spaceship in my yard while I was doing my homework.

5. Grandma and Grandpa _____ _____ a sandcastle at the beach.

6. The cat and the fiddle _____ _____ in the moonlight.

Word Bank	
were sailing	were building
were dancing	were landing
were working	were singing

Homework: ❏ Say each *were verb+ing* combination in your own sentence.

❏ _____.

_____ _____ _____
Name　　　　　　　　Homework Partner　　　　　Date

Were Verb+ing

Activity Card

Were Verb+ing

Tell your homework partner in a complete sentence:

1. Tell what the stars were doing last night.

2. Where were the stars twinkling last night?

_____
Name

_____
Date

Activity Card

Were Verb+ing

Tell your homework partner in a complete sentence:

1. Tell what your class was playing at recess.

2. Tell where your class was playing at recess.

_____
Name

_____
Date

Activity Card

Were Verb+ing

Tell your homework partner in a complete sentence:

1. Tell where you and your friends were eating lunch.

2. Tell what you and your friends were eating for lunch.

_____
Name

_____
Date

Activity Card

Were Verb+ing

Tell your homework partner in a complete sentence:

1. Tell what you and your friends were hoping would happen today.

2. Tell when you and your friends were hoping for something to happen today.

_____
Name

_____
Date

Were Verb+ing

#BK-309 Grammar Tickle Stories™ • ©2004 Super Duper® Publications • 1-800-277-8737 • Online! www.superduperinc.com

Were Verb+ing

Tell your homework partner in a complete sentence:

1. Tell where the students were throwing their trash after lunch today.

2. Tell why the students were throwing their trash away after lunch today.

Name _____

Date _____

Were Verb+ing

Finish these sentences:

1. My parents were talking about _____.

2. My parents were laughing about _____.

Name _____

Date _____

Were Verb+ing

Tell your homework partner in a complete sentence:

1. Tell where the students were parking their bikes at school.

2. Tell when the students were parking their bikes at school.

Name _____

Date _____

Were Verb+ing

Finish these sentences:

1. We were planning a trip to _____.

2. We were writing a story about _____.

Name _____

Date _____

Were Verb+ing

The Hare and Tortoise Explain

Directions: Give each student a list of the Picture Words on pages 112 and 123 or the Word Lists on pages 113 and 124. Do not reveal the story title. Ask the student for "words" from his/her page to fill in the spaces in the story below. Write the words in the spaces. You may also have the student write these words on his/her Companion Activity Sheet (page 139). Then, have the student read/listen to the story. For more options, see *How To Use This Book* on page ii.

(The Hare says it happened this way.)

Okay, it was like this. The Tortoise _____ down by the
(was verb+ing)

watering hole yesterday, while the other animals _____. He saw
(were verb+ing)

me coming and decided to get moving. Later, he _____ down by
(was verb+ing)

the old tree when he stopped to have a chat with me. We _____
(were verb+ing)

nicely when all of a sudden I fell asleep. What did he do? He took off!

(The Tortoise explains his version of the story.)

Uh, this is how it happened. You see, uh, the Hare _____
(was verb+ing)

while the other animals _____ down by the entrance to the forest.
(were verb+ing)

Uh, the Hare yawned and felt sleepy, so while he _____, I just
(was verb+ing)

kept going and finished the race. When I got to the finish line, the other animals

_____ and woke him up. Boy, was he hopping mad!
(were verb+ing)

Questions: (Answer in a complete sentence.)

❏ 1. What does the Hare say the Tortoise was doing?

❏ 2. What does the Hare say they were doing when he fell asleep?

❏ 3. What does the Tortoise say the Hare was doing?

❏ 4. What does the Tortoise say the other animals were doing by the entrance of the forest?

❏ 5. What does the Tortoise say the animals were doing when the Hare woke up?

Homework: Take a copy of this story and word/picture list home, and follow the directions above.

Name	Homework Partner	Date

Was / Were Verb+ing Combo

#BK-309 Grammar Tickle Stories™ • ©2004 Super Duper® Publications • 1-800-277-8737 • Online! www.superduperinc.com

A Short Poem

Directions: Give each student a list of the Picture Words on pages 112 and 123 or the Word Lists on pages 113 and 124. Do not reveal the story title. Ask the student for "words" from his/her page to fill in the spaces in the story below. Write the words in the spaces. You may also have the student write these words on his/her Companion Activity Sheet (page 139). Then, have the student read/listen to the story. For more options, see *How To Use This Book* on page ii.

Claire _____ in the garden.   Ned _____ in the house.
　　　　　　(was verb+ing)　　　　　　　　　　　　　　　　　　　　(was verb+ing)

They _____ together, and were quiet as a mouse!
　　　　(were verb+ing)

They _____ up a secret for their Momma's special day,
　　　　(were verb+ing)

while she _____ in the kitchen, having left them to their play.
　　　　　　(was verb+ing)

Dad came in and said "Hello" and wondered why it was so quiet.

"They _____ last I knew. I made pudding, come and try it!"
　　　　(were verb+ing)

Dad _____ when he heard, "Mom, close your eyes."
　　　(was verb+ing)

They walked in with a card they made, and yelled out "Mom, Surprise!"

Claire and Ned _____ . Mom said, "You've made me feel so glad!
　　　　　　　　　(were verb+ing)

This is the greatest birthday gift I've ever had."

Questions: (Answer in a complete sentence.)

❑ 1. What does the poem say Claire was doing in the garden?
❑ 2. What does the poem say Ned was doing in the house?
❑ 3. What does the poem say Ned and Claire were doing together as quiet as a mouse?
❑ 4. What does the poem say mom was doing in the kitchen?
❑ 5. What does mom say after Claire and Ned yell surprise?

Homework: Take a copy of this story and word/picture list home, and follow the directions above.

_____ 　　 _____ 　　 _____
Name 　　　　　　　　　　　　 Homework Partner 　　　　　　　　　Date

Was / Were Verb+ing Combo

She Was Comin' Round The Mountain

Directions: Give each student a list of the Picture Words on pages 112 and 123 or the Word Lists on pages 113 and 124. Do not reveal the story title. Ask the student for "words" from his/her page to fill in the spaces in the story below. Write the words in the spaces. You may also have the student write these words on his/her Companion Activity Sheet (page 139). Then, have the student read/listen to the story. For more options, see *How To Use This Book* on page ii.

Do you remember the song *She'll Be Coming Round The Mountain*? Well, I can't

remember why she was coming around the mountain, but this is the story I heard. Once

upon a time, Maude Cooper _____. The people in the town
 (was verb+ing)

_____ and waiting for her to get to the town. The storekeeper
 (were verb+ing)

_____, and the sheriff and his deputy _____.
 (was verb+ing)   (were verb+ing)

Well, the day got long, and the sun got hot. To pass the time, the people started singing.

The school teacher _____ and all of the choir singers
 (was verb+ing)

_____. But where in the world was Maude? Finally, as the sun
 (were verb+ing)

_____ , Maude came riding into town driving six white horses. The
 (was verb+ing)

horses _____. They all went out to greet her when she arrived.
 (were verb+ing)

Maude, pink pajamas and all, had finally come around the mountain. They heard her say

that she came to town to buy a new outfit!

Questions: (Answer in a complete sentence.)

❏ 1. What was Maude Cooper doing?
❏ 2. What were people in the town doing?
❏ 3. What was the storekeeper doing?
❏ 4. What were the sheriff and his deputy doing?
❏ 5. What was the sun doing?

Homework: Take a copy of this story and word/picture list home, and follow the directions above.

_____   _____   _____
        Name   Homework Partner   Date

| Was / Were |
| Verb+ing |
| Combo |

The People On The Bus

Directions: Give each student a list of the Picture Words on pages 112 and 123 or the Word Lists on pages 113 and 124. Do not reveal the story title. Ask the student for "words" from his/her page to fill in the spaces in the story below. Write the words in the spaces. You may also have the student write these words on his/her Companion Activity Sheet (page 139). Then, have the student read/listen to the story. For more options, see *How To Use This Book* on page ii.

As told by the driver (when he was pulled over by a police officer).

Police Officer: "Good afternoon, sir, I saw that you _____ so I decided
(were verb+ing)

to pull you over and check it out."

Driver: "Hello Officer. Well, you see, here is the problem. The people on the bus

_____ up and down all through the town."
(were verb+ing)

Police Officer: "From what I could see, the horn on the bus _____
(was verb+ing)

beep, beep, beep, all through the town."

Driver: "I think that the door _____ all through the town. Then, the
(was verb+ing)

wheels _____ all through the town."
(were verb+ing)

Police Officer: "I heard a lot of noise."

Driver: "Yes, Officer, I'm sorry, but the babies _____ all through the
(were verb+ing)

town too. The money _____ and that goes *clink, clink, clink!*"
(was verb+ing)

Police Officer: "So what did you do?"

Driver: "Well, I _____, and that's when you pulled me over!"
(was verb+ing)

Questions: (Answer in a complete sentence.)
- ❏ 1. What does the driver say the people on the bus were doing?
- ❏ 2. What does the officer say the horn on the bus was doing?
- ❏ 3. What does the driver say the wheels were doing?
- ❏ 4. What does the driver say the babies were doing?
- ❏ 5. What does the driver say he was doing when the officer pulled him over?

Homework: Take a copy of this story and word/picture list home, and follow the directions above.

_____   _____   _____

Name   Homework Partner   Date

**Was / Were
Verb+ing
Combo**

Cinderella Having A Ball

Directions: Give each student a list of the Picture Words on pages 112 and 123 or the Word Lists on pages 113 and 124. Do not reveal the story title. Ask each student for "words" from his/her page to fill in the spaces in the story below. Write the words in the spaces. You may also have the student write these words on his/her Companion Activity Sheet (page 139). Then, have the student read/listen to the story. For more options, see *How To Use This Book* on page ii.

This is Frank Lee Tellingyou with *Castle News,* reporting live from the prince's castle.

Shortly after midnight, Cinderella disappeared. Eyewitnesses report that people

_____ all evening. When Cinderella arrived, the band
     (were verb+ing)

_____, and everyone stopped. The Prince _____
     (was verb+ing)   (was verb+ing)

when he came over to her. Cinderella's mean stepsisters _____.
                                                     (were verb+ing)

They didn't recognize her. The King and Queen _____ as the
                                           (were verb+ing)

Prince took Cinderella's hand. The orchestra leader _____ and
                                              (was verb+ing)

the music began. The stars _____. There was magic in the air.
                               (were verb+ing)

Suddenly, the clock struck midnight and Cinderella _____.
                                               (was verb+ing)

Now the big question is: Where in the world is Cinderella?

If you have any information on where Cinderella might be, call this station immediately.

This is Frank Lee Tellingyou reporting for *Castle News!*

Questions: (Answer in a complete sentence.)
- ❏ 1. What do eyewitnesses report that people were doing all evening?
- ❏ 2. What was the band doing when Cinderella arrived?
- ❏ 3. What was the Prince doing when Cinderella arrived?
- ❏ 4. What were the King and Queen doing?
- ❏ 5. What were the stars doing?

Homework: Take a copy of this story and word/picture list home, and follow the directions above.

_____   _____   _____
Name   Homework Partner   Date

Was / Were Verb+ing Combo

#BK-309 Grammar Tickle Stories™ • ©2004 Super Duper® Publications • 1-800-277-8737 • Online! www.superduperinc.com

Was/Were Verb+ing Combo Companion Activity Sheet

Directions: During or following the story, have the student write words from the word or picture list on the lines below. Then, have the student write sentences with these words in them.

Example: _____ ***was barking*** _____   - OR -   _____ ***were shopping*** _____

*Last night, my dog **was barking** very loudly.   Yesterday, we **were shopping** all afternoon.*

1. _____

_____

2. _____

_____

3. _____

_____

4. _____

_____

5. _____

_____

6. _____

_____

7. _____

_____

8. _____

_____

Homework: ❑ Take a copy of this sheet home with a word/picture list. Then, follow the directions above.

_____ _____ _____

| | | | **Was / Were Verb+ing Combo** |

Name   Homework Partner   Date

Who Was? They Were!

Directions: Read these sentences and decide which word (WAS or WERE) is missing and circle it in the columns on the right, or write it on the line.

1. Maude _____ driving six white horses when she

   came around the mountain.   **was**   **were**

2. Ned and Claire _____ planting a vegetable garden.   **was**   **were**

3. The Hare _____ sleeping when the Tortoise passed him.   **was**   **were**

4. The animals at the finish line _____ cheering for

   the winner.   **was**   **were**

5. The driver on the bus _____ driving people to the city. **was**   **were**

6. The wheels on the bus _____ going round and round.   **was**   **were**

7. Cinderella and the Prince _____ dancing when the clock

   struck midnight.   **was**   **were**

8. The band _____ playing a special song for Cinderella

   and the Prince.   **was**   **were**

Homework: ❏ Say each was/were verb+ing combination in your own sentence.

❏ _____.

_____   _____   _____
         Name   Homework Partner   Date

Was / Were Verb+ing Combo

#BK-309 Grammar Tickle Stories™ • ©2004 Super Duper® Publications • 1-800-277-8737 • Online! www.superduperinc.com

Activity Card

Was/Were Verb+ing Combo

Fill in the blanks with a was or were and verb+ing combination (for example, "was talking"). Answer in a complete sentence.

1. They _____ at the stars last night.

2. He _____ on the brightest star for a new bike.

Name _____

Date _____

Activity Card

Was/Were Verb+ing Combo

Fill in the blanks with a was or were and verb+ing combination (for example, "was talking"). Answer in a complete sentence.

1. We _____ popcorn and watching a movie.

2. The butter _____ in the pot to pour over them.

Name _____

Date _____

Activity Card

Was/Were Verb+ing Combo

Fill in the blanks with a was or were and verb+ing combination (for example, "was talking"). Answer in a complete sentence.

1. I _____ my teeth this morning.

2. You _____ your teeth this morning.

Name _____

Date _____

Activity Card

Was/Were Verb+ing Combo

Fill in the blanks with a was or were and verb+ing combination (for example, "was talking"). Answer in a complete sentence.

1. The juggler _____ the balls in the air.

2. The balls _____ on the ground, when he didn't catch them.

Name _____

Date _____

Was / Were Verb+ing

Was/Were Verb+ing Combo

Fill in the blanks with a was or were and verb+ing combination (for example, "was talking"). Answer in a complete sentence.

1. The ballerina _____ on _____ her toes during the recital.

2. The people _____ to let _____ her know she was doing a good job.

Name _____

Date _____

Was/Were Verb+ing Combo

Fill in the blanks with a was or were and verb+ing combination (for example, "was talking"). Answer in a complete sentence.

1. The climbers _____ a _____ high mountain last weekend.

2. One climber _____ to rest _____ when the others said, "that's a good idea!"

Name _____

Date _____

Was/Were Verb+ing Combo

Fill in the blanks with a was or were and verb+ing combination (for example, "was talking"). Answer in a complete sentence.

1. The skiers _____ down _____ the mountain together.

2. One skier _____, "I lost _____ my pole," to the other skiers.

Name _____

Date _____

Was/Were Verb+ing Combo

Fill in the blanks with a was or were and verb+ing combination (for example, "was talking"). Answer in a complete sentence.

1. It _____ so I got out _____ my umbrella.

2. The rain drops _____ on my nose!

Name _____

Date _____

Was / Were Verb+ing Combo

#BK-309 Grammar Tickle Stories™ • ©2004 Super Duper® Publications • 1-800-277-8737 • Online! www.superduperinc.com

Regular and Irregular Past Tense Verbs

Regular Past Tense Verbs

Directions: Use the picture words below to help you complete the stories on pages 146 to 150 and 166 to 170.

brush**ed**

cook**ed**

jump**ed**

rak**ed**

carri**ed**

cri**ed**

kick**ed**

shar**ed**

clapp**ed**

danc**ed**

knock**ed**

skat**ed**

clean**ed**

dri**ed**

lick**ed**

skipp**ed**

climb**ed**

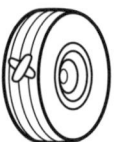

fix**ed**

paint**ed**

ti**ed**

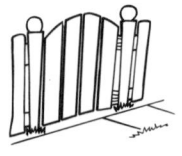

clos**ed**

hugg**ed**

plant**ed**

wash**ed**

#BK-309 Grammar Tickle Stories™ • ©2004 Super Duper® Publications • 1-800-277-8737 • Online! www.superduperinc.com

Regular Past Tense Verbs

Directions: Use these words to help complete the stories on pages 146 to 150 and 166 to 170.

❏ baked	❏ knocked	❏ served
❏ borrowed	❏ learned	❏ shared
❏ brushed	❏ licked	❏ shaved
❏ buttoned	❏ lifted	❏ shined
❏ carried	❏ listened	❏ shopped
❏ chased	❏ looked	❏ shouted
❏ clapped	❏ mailed	❏ skated
❏ cleaned	❏ moved	❏ skipped
❏ climbed	❏ mowed	❏ smiled
❏ closed	❏ opened	❏ snowed
❏ cooked	❏ packed	❏ splashed
❏ crawled	❏ painted	❏ started
❏ cried	❏ parked	❏ stopped
❏ danced	❏ planted	❏ studied
❏ dressed	❏ played	❏ surprised
❏ dried	❏ poured	❏ tasted
❏ dropped	❏ pulled	❏ tickled
❏ fixed	❏ pushed	❏ tied
❏ floated	❏ rained	❏ turned
❏ growled	❏ raked	❏ visited
❏ guessed	❏ reached	❏ waited
❏ hammered	❏ roared	❏ walked
❏ helped	❏ rocked	❏ washed
❏ hopped	❏ rolled	❏ watched
❏ hugged	❏ sailed	❏ whistled
❏ jumped	❏ scooped	❏ worked
❏ kicked	❏ scored	❏ zipped

Regular Past
Tense Verbs

My Summer Trip

Directions: Give each student a list of the Picture Words on page 144 or the Word List on page 145. Do not reveal the story title. Ask the student for "words" from his/her page to fill in the spaces in the story below. Write the words in the spaces. You may also have the student write these words on his/her Companion Activity Sheet (page 151). Then, have the student read/listen to the story. For more options, see *How To Use This Book* on page ii.

It was the first day of September. The fourth grade class _____ to school
(regular past tense verb)

from summer vacation. On the board they saw, "Today we will read *My Summer Trip*

papers." Everyone _____ when their teacher, Mrs. Smart, said "Each one of
(regular past tense verb)

you please get up and read one thing from your paper." First, Billy said, "I _____
(regular past tense verb)

all summer and it was fun!" Then, Jeannie said, "I only _____ last week."
(regular past tense verb)

Greta, Rosanna and Victor all _____, but not together. "What did you do Mrs.
(regular past tense verb)

Smart?" they all asked. "This is not my writing assignment," she laughed. Then she said,

"The first week of vacation, I just _____ in my rose garden. It was very
(regular past tense verb)

relaxing! The second week I _____. Then, I said to myself, 'Mrs. Smart, you're
(regular past tense verb)

on vacation, you need to have some fun!' So, I _____." The
(regular past tense verb)

class applauded. They thought she was very "Smart".

Today we will read My Summer Trip papers.

Questions: (Answer in a complete sentence.)
- ❏ 1. What did everyone do when Mrs. Smart said they'd each have to read one thing?
- ❏ 2. What did Billy do all summer?
- ❏ 3. What did Greta, Rosanna and Victor all do?
- ❏ 4. What did Mrs. Smart do the first week of her vacation?
- ❏ 5. What did Mrs. Smart do the day she decided she needed to have some fun?

Homework: Take a copy of this story and word/picture list home, and follow the directions above.

_____ _____ _____
Name   Homework Partner   Date

Regular Past Tense Verbs

#BK-309 Grammar Tickle Stories™ • ©2004 Super Duper® Publications • 1-800-277-8737 • Online! www.superduperinc.com

Stuffed Animal Factory Visit

Directions: Give each student a list of the Picture Words on page 144 or the Word List on page 145. Do not reveal the story title. Ask the student for "words" from his/her page to fill in the spaces in the story below. Write the words in the spaces. You may also have the student write these words on his/her Companion Activity Sheet (page 151). Then, have the student read/listen to the story. For more options, see *How To Use This Book* on page ii.

Dear Aunt Mildred and Uncle Mo,

Yesterday, my class went to the stuffed animal factory. We got on the school bus and

we _____ the whole way there! Our teacher _____ the
    (regular past tense verb)   (regular past tense verb)

whole time because we were having so much fun! When we got there, the tour guide

_____ and showed us where the animals _____. Once we
(regular past tense verb)   (regular past tense verb)

chose the one we wanted (I chose a dog just like my dog, Ralph), we went to the stuffing

room, where they _____. Next, we went to the outfit room. We watched
                      (regular past tense verb)

as the outfits were _____. The hats had just been _____. I
             (regular past tense verb)   (regular past tense verb)

chose a blue one! We were all excited. We got back on the bus and

_____ until we got back to school. Please come visit us and see my new
(regular past tense verb)

stuffed dog (and Ralph, too)!

Love,

Natty

Questions: (Answer in a complete sentence.)
- ❏ 1. What did Natty say they did on the way to the factory?
- ❏ 2. What did Natty say her teacher did on the bus the whole time?
- ❏ 3. What did the tour guide do when they got there?
- ❏ 4. What did Natty say about the hats in the hat room?
- ❏ 5. What did Natty say the students did all the way back to school?

Homework: Take a copy of this story and word/picture list home, and follow the directions above.

			Regular Past Tense Verbs
Name	Homework Partner	Date	

Penguin Day

Directions: Give each student a list of the Picture Words on page 144 or the Word List on page 145. Do not reveal the story title. Ask the student for "words" from his/her page to fill in the spaces in the story below. Write the words in the spaces. You may also have the student write these words on his/her Companion Activity Sheet (page 151). Then, have the student read/listen to the story. For more options, see *How To Use This Book* on page ii.

This week we are going to study about penguins. Then, on Friday, we'll all dress up

in black and white and have *Penguin Day*. Let me tell you something about these

interesting birds. Penguins _____ many years ago. They never
(regular past tense verb)

_____, not even millions of years ago. Then, as time went by, they
(regular past tense verb)

_____. It is well known that penguins _____ in water, even
(regular past tense verb)   (regular past tense verb)

though they _____ on land. They learned to waddle long before they
(regular past tense verb)

_____. Their wings _____, and this helped them. Penguins
(regular past tense verb)   (regular past tense verb)

had short, thick feathers because they _____ in very cold climates. Now
(regular past tense verb)

you know a lot more about penguins. Everyone stand up, and let's practice waddling!

Questions: (Answer in a complete sentence.)

❑ 1. What did penguins do many years ago?

❑ 2. What have penguins never done even millions of years ago?

❑ 3. What did penguins do in water?

❑ 4. What did penguins do on land?

❑ 5. What did penguins learn to do long after they learned to waddle?

Homework: Take a copy of this story and word/picture list home, and follow the directions above.

_____   _____   _____
Name   Homework Partner   Date

Regular Past Tense Verbs

#BK-309 Grammar Tickle Stories™ • ©2004 Super Duper® Publications • 1-800-277-8737 • Online! www.superduperinc.com

Spider Man

Directions: Give each student a list of the Picture Words on page 144 or the Word List on page 145. Do not reveal the story title. Ask the student for "words" from his/her page to fill in the spaces in the story below. Write the words in the spaces. You may also have the student write these words on his/her Companion Activity Sheet (page 151). Then, have the student read/listen to the story. For more options, see *How To Use This Book* on page ii.

Yesterday, we had a visit from the Spider Man. No, not the kind in books and movies!

He was from the local museum. He told us lots of interesting things about the history of

spiders. For instance, spiders _____ long before they spun webs. They
(regular past tense verb)

_____ for hours and would get very tired. When they wanted to catch their
(regular past tense verb)

prey, they _____. When spiders first began spinning webs, they
(regular past tense verb)

_____ other insects into them. Not all spiders were dangerous. Many
(regular past tense verb)

spiders _____, which helped farmers and saved crops. While he talked, the
(regular past tense verb)

Spider Man showed us a spider. He told us, "Once, this spider _____, and
(regular past tense verb)

I'd never seen one do that! I _____ and walked away." The most interesting
(regular past tense verb)

fact I learned about spiders is that they _____. But, my Mom still won't let
(regular past tense verb)

me have one for a pet.

Questions: (Answer in a complete sentence.)
- ❏ 1. What did the Spider Man say spiders did long before they spun webs?
- ❏ 2. What did spiders do for hours that made them tired?
- ❏ 3. What did spiders do when they wanted to catch their prey?
- ❏ 4. What did spiders do that helped farmers and saved crops?
- ❏ 5. What did the Spider Man say he did before walking away from the spider?

Homework: Take a copy of this story and word/picture list home, and follow the directions above.

_____ _____ _____ **Regular Past Tense Verbs**
Name   Homework Partner   Date

If Only I'd Stayed In Bed, By Little Red

Directions: Give each student a list of the Picture Words on page 144 or the Word List on page 145. Do not reveal the story title. Ask the student for "words" from his/her page to fill in the spaces in the story below. Write the words in the spaces. You may also have the student write these words on his/her Companion Activity Sheet (page 151). Then, have the student read/listen to the story. For more options, see *How To Use This Book* on page ii.

If only I'd stayed in bed that day, instead of going to Grandma's house, everything

would be different. I wouldn't have _____ in the woods and picked

(regular past tense verb)

flowers. I might not have _____ with that basket of food. I certainly

(regular past tense verb)

wouldn't have _____ when I saw the Wolf! If I hadn't told the Wolf where I

(regular past tense verb)

was going, then he wouldn't have _____ and gone to my grandma's house

(regular past tense verb)

first. When I got there, and he was disguised as Grandma, I wouldn't have

_____. I should have noticed what big eyes, ears, nose, and mouth he

(regular past tense verb)

had! When I did notice these things, I _____. The Woodsman came

(regular past tense verb)

running. He _____ and then the Wolf ran into the woods. If only I'd

(regular past tense verb)

_____ that day instead. But if I had done that, you would never have

(regular past tense verb)

heard the story of *Little Red Riding Hood*!

Questions: (Answer in a complete sentence.)
- ❏ 1. What did Little Red say she wouldn't have done in the woods?
- ❏ 2. What did Little Red say she wouldn't have done with the basket of food?
- ❏ 3. What did Little Red say the Wolf wouldn't have done if she hadn't talked to him?
- ❏ 4. What did Little Red do when she noticed the Wolf's big eyes?
- ❏ 5. What did the woodsman do to scare the Wolf?

Homework: Take a copy of this story and word/picture list home, and follow the directions above.

_____ _____ _____

Name　　　　　　　　Homework Partner　　　　　　　　Date

Regular Past Tense Verbs

#BK-309 Grammar Tickle Stories™ • ©2004 Super Duper® Publications • 1-800-277-8737 • Online! www.superduperinc.com

Regular Past Tense Verbs Companion Activity Sheet

Directions: During or following the story, have the student write words from the word or picture list on the lines below. Then, have the student write sentences with these words in them.

Example: _____ ***clapped*** _____

The fans **clapped** after the team scored a touchdown.

1. _____

_____

2. _____

_____

3. _____

_____

4. _____

_____

5. _____

_____

6. _____

_____

7. _____

_____

8. _____

_____

Homework: ❏ Take a copy of this sheet home with a word/picture list. Then, follow the directions above.

_____ _____ _____

Name   Homework Partner   Date

Regular Past Tense Verbs

Mended Sentences

Directions: Help fix these mixed up sentences by choosing the correct word from the words/pictures below. Cross out the wrong word and write, or have a helper write, the correct word on the line.

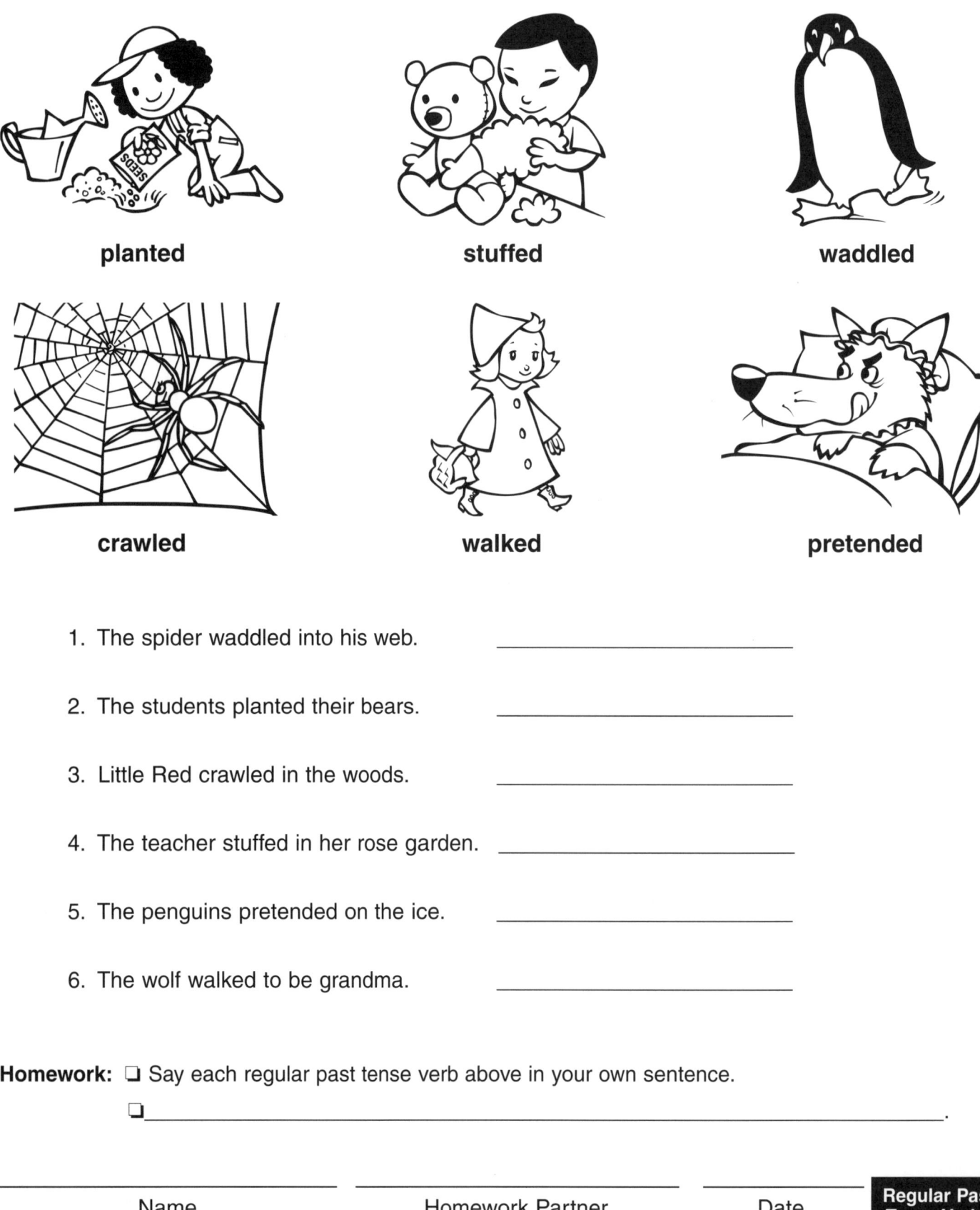

planted   **stuffed**   **waddled**

crawled   **walked**   **pretended**

1. The spider waddled into his web.   _____

2. The students planted their bears.   _____

3. Little Red crawled in the woods.   _____

4. The teacher stuffed in her rose garden.   _____

5. The penguins pretended on the ice.   _____

6. The wolf walked to be grandma.   _____

Homework: ❏ Say each regular past tense verb above in your own sentence.

❏_____.

_____   _____   _____
Name   Homework Partner   Date

**Regular Past
Tense Verbs**

#BK-309 Grammar Tickle Stories™ • ©2004 Super Duper® Publications • 1-800-277-8737 • Online! www.superduperinc.com

Regular Past Tense Verbs

Tell your homework partner in a complete sentence:

1. Tell what you studied in school today.

2. Tell where you studied in school today.

(Bonus Activity: Close your eyes, and then tell what you just did.)

_____ _____
Name   Date

Regular Past Tense Verbs

Tell your homework partner in a complete sentence:

1. Tell what you used to wash your face.

2. Tell when you washed your face.

(Bonus Activity: Cross your fingers, and then tell what you just did.)

_____ _____
Name   Date

Regular Past Tense Verbs

Tell your homework partner in a complete sentence:

1. Tell when you brushed your teeth.

2. Tell why you brushed your teeth.

(Bonus Activity: Wiggle your nose, and then tell what you just did.)

_____ _____
Name   Date

Regular Past Tense Verbs

Tell your homework partner in a complete sentence:

1. Tell what you played at recess.

2. Tell who you played with at recess.

(Bonus Activity: Hop on one foot, and then tell what you just did.)

_____ _____
Name   Date

Regular Past Tense Verbs

Regular Past Tense Verbs

Tell your homework partner in a complete sentence:

1. Tell when you helped someone.

2. Tell why they needed your help.

(Bonus Activity: Pick something up off the floor, and then tell what you just did.)

_____ Date

_____ Name

Regular Past Tense Verbs

Tell your homework partner in a complete sentence:

1. Tell what you smiled about.

2. Tell why you smiled.

(Bonus Activity: Smile, and then tell what you just did.)

_____ Date

_____ Name

Regular Past Tense Verbs

Tell your homework partner in a complete sentence:

1. Tell what you buttoned, zipped, or tied today.

2. Tell where you buttoned, zipped, or tied today.

(Bonus Activity: Zip or tie something, and then tell what you just did.)

_____ Date

_____ Name

Regular Past Tense Verbs

Tell your homework partner in a complete sentence:

1. Tell about something you opened.

2. Tell about something you closed.

(Bonus Activity: Open the refrigerator, and then tell what you just did.)

_____ Date

_____ Name

Regular Past Tense Verbs

Irregular Past Tense Verbs

Directions: Use the picture words below to help you complete the stories on pages 157 to 161 and 166 to 170.

ate	dove	flew	swam
blew	drank	hit	swept
broke	drew	ran	thought
built	drove	rode	threw
caught	dug	sang	won
cut	fell	slid	wrote

Irregular Past Tense Verbs

Directions: Use these words to help complete the stories on pages 157 to 161 and 166 to 170.

❏ ate	❏ got	❏ shrank
❏ beat	❏ grew	❏ slept
❏ began	❏ had	❏ slid
❏ bent	❏ heard	❏ sold
❏ bit	❏ held	❏ spent
❏ blew	❏ hid	❏ spoke
❏ bought	❏ hit	❏ spread
❏ broke	❏ kept	❏ spun
❏ brought	❏ knelt	❏ stole
❏ built	❏ knew	❏ stood
❏ came	❏ laid	❏ struck
❏ caught	❏ led	❏ strung
❏ chose	❏ left	❏ swam
❏ cost	❏ lent	❏ swept
❏ crept	❏ lit	❏ swung
❏ cut	❏ lost	❏ taught
❏ did	❏ made	❏ thought
❏ dove	❏ meant	❏ threw
❏ drank	❏ met	❏ told
❏ dreamt	❏ paid	❏ took
❏ drew	❏ ran	❏ tore
❏ drove	❏ rang	❏ went
❏ dug	❏ read	❏ wept
❏ fed	❏ rode	❏ wet
❏ fell	❏ rose	❏ woke
❏ felt	❏ said	❏ won
❏ flew	❏ sang	❏ wore
❏ forgot	❏ sank	❏ wove
❏ fought	❏ sat	❏ wrote
❏ found	❏ saw	
❏ froze	❏ sent	
❏ gave	❏ shook	

Irregular Past
Tense Verbs

#BK-309 Grammar Tickle Stories™ • ©2004 Super Duper® Publications • 1-800-277-8737 • Online! www.superduperinc.com

The Ole' Ball Game

Directions: Give each student a list of the Picture Words on page 155 or the Word List on page 156. Do not reveal the story title. Ask the student for "words" from his/her page to fill in the spaces in the story below. Write the words in the spaces. You may also have the student write these words on his/her Companion Activity Sheet (page 162). Then, have the student read/listen to the story. For more options, see *How To Use This Book* on page ii.

𝔗𝔥𝔢 𝔇𝔞𝔦𝔩𝔶 𝔊𝔬𝔬𝔡 𝔖𝔭𝔬𝔯𝔱

Yesterday's ball game, between the *Lightening Strikers* and the *Big Bats,* was one of

the most exciting games in Little League History. The game was tied 7-7 in the 9th

inning. Johnny Riggs, of the *Big Bats,* was up first. He _____ and missed.

(irregular past tense verb)

But on his next turn, he _____ and got to second base. The pitcher

(irregular past tense verb)

_____ and called a time out. The next batter was Powerhouse Pete. You

(irregular past tense verb)

could tell he was going to be tough because, as he came to the plate, he

_____ and everyone gasped! Pete _____ the ball right up to

(irregular past tense verb)   (irregular past tense verb)

the fence and Johnny ran home. The third baseman _____, but it was too

(irregular past tense verb)

late. The score was 9-7. Now, *Lightening Strikers* were up. The first three players got on

base to load the bases. Then, the next three batters _____. The *Big Bats*

(irregular past tense verb)

won! The crowd _____. Yes, sports fans, it was quite a day for baseball!

(irregular past tense verb)

Questions: (Answer in a complete sentence.)

- ❑ 1. What did Johnny Riggs do the first time at bat?
- ❑ 2. What did Powerhouse Pete do before he came to the plate?
- ❑ 3. What did the pitcher do?
- ❑ 4. What did the third baseman do, but was too late?
- ❑ 5. What did the crowd do when *Big Bats* won?

Homework: Take a copy of this story and word/picture list home, and follow the directions above.

_____   _____   _____

Name   Homework Partner   Date

Irregular Past Tense Verbs

Bird Watching

Directions: Give each student a list of the Picture Words on page 155 or the Word List on page 156. Do not reveal the story title. Ask the student for "words" from his/her page to fill in the spaces in the story below. Write the words in the spaces. You may also have the student write these words on his/her Companion Activity Sheet (page 162). Then, have the student read/listen to the story. For more options, see *How To Use This Book* on page ii.

Yesterday the *Big Beak Bird Watchers* went on their annual retreat. They

_____ for three hours into the woods until they _____
(irregular past tense verb)   (irregular past tense verb)

the calling of the *Fleet Footed Flooty Bird*. It almost sounded like it said

"_____," as it sang out its call. Club members _____ the
(irregular past tense verb)   (irregular past tense verb)

birds while looking through their high powered binoculars. "The better to see them

with, my dears!" said one of the members. Another member exclaimed, "I

_____ one!" Later in the day, after everyone _____, they
(irregular past tense verb)   (irregular past tense verb)

took a short rest. They all _____ around a campfire before heading
(irregular past tense verb)

home. One watcher summed up everyone's feelings. "I never knew what I had

missed before. I am so glad that I _____ these birds."
(irregular past tense verb)

Questions: (Answer in a complete sentence.)

❑ 1. What did the bird watchers do for three hours?

❑ 2. What did it sound like the *Fleet Footed Flooty* said?

❑ 3. What did everyone do before they took a rest?

❑ 4. What did the club members do around the campfire?

❑ 5. What did one member say that summed up how everyone felt?

Homework: Take a copy of this story and word/picture list home, and follow the directions above.

Name	Homework Partner	Date

Irregular Past Tense Verbs

#BK-309 Grammar Tickle Stories™ • ©2004 Super Duper® Publications • 1-800-277-8737 • Online! www.superduperinc.com

Going Up!

Directions: Give each student a list of the Picture Words on page 155 or the Word List on page 156. Do not reveal the story title. Ask the student for "words" from his/her page to fill in the spaces in the story below. Write the words in the spaces. You may also have the student write these words on his/her Companion Activity Sheet (page 162). Then, have the student read/listen to the story. For more options, see *How To Use This Book* on page ii.

The new *Mighty Mall* building was open to the public for the first time today. When he

was asked how he _____ it, the builder said, "First, the architect

(irregular past tense verb)

_____ the plans. We went over them and _____ some

(irregular past tense verb)   (irregular past tense verb)

changes. Once that was done, we hired the workers. They _____ very

                                                        (irregular past tense verb)

hard. One crew _____ the beams that hold up this enormous structure.

                 (irregular past tense verb)

Another crew _____ the foundation you're standing on. At the end, the

                 (irregular past tense verb)

designers _____ the beautiful colors and patterns you see inside the

             (irregular past tense verb)

building." When asked if he would do such a huge job again, the builder said, "I

_____ this job and would gladly do it again!"

(irregular past tense verb)

Questions: (Answer in a complete sentence.)

- ❏ 1. What did the builder say the architect did?
- ❏ 2. What did the builder say the workers did very hard?
- ❏ 3. What did the builder say that the first crew did to the beam?
- ❏ 4. What did the builder say the designers did?
- ❏ 5. What did the builder say when asked if he would do such a huge job again?

Homework: Take a copy of this story and word/picture list home, and follow the directions above.

Name   Homework Partner   Date   **Irregular Past Tense Verbs**

Real Troopers

Directions: Give each student a list of the Picture Words on page 155 or the Word List on page 156. Do not reveal the story title. Ask the student for "words" from his/her page to fill in the spaces in the story below. Write the words in the spaces. You may also have the student write these words on his/her Companion Activity Sheet (page 162). Then, have the student read/listen to the story. For more options, see *How To Use This Book* on page ii.

Scout Sales Report

This year, I'm happy to report that we _____ more cookies than ever
(irregular past tense verb)

before! *Troop 16* went to the supermarket every Saturday and _____ with
(irregular past tense verb)

people to get them to buy cookies. *Troop 111* held a talent show and people

_____ cookies at intermission, paying 50 cents for two. *Troop 2* held a car
(irregular past tense verb)

wash. For five dollars, they _____ the outside of the car and
(irregular past tense verb)

_____ the inside. They also threw in a box of cookies, as an extra
(irregular past tense verb)

surprise! One customer said, "My car _____ after that!" The *Troop 2*
(irregular past tense verb)

leader said, "I've never _____ scouts so dedicated." After we
(irregular past tense verb)

_____ , she took us all out for ice cream!
(irregular past tense verb)

Questions: (Answer in a complete sentence.)

- ❏ 1. What did *Troop 16* do to get people to buy cookies?
- ❏ 2. What did *Troop 2* do to the outside of each car they washed?
- ❏ 3. What did *Troop 2* do to the inside of each car they washed?
- ❏ 4. What did one customer say about the car?
- ❏ 5. What did the troop leader say about her troop?

Homework: Take a copy of this story and word/picture list home, and follow the directions above.

_____   _____   _____
Name   Homework Partner   Date

Irregular Past Tense Verbs

#BK-309 Grammar Tickle Stories™ • ©2004 Super Duper® Publications • 1-800-277-8737 • Online! www.superduperinc.com

Sleepy's Tale

Directions: Give each student a list of the Picture Words on page 155 or the Word List on page 156. Do not reveal the story title. Ask the student for "words" from his/her page to fill in the spaces in the story below. Write the words in the spaces. You may also have the student write these words on his/her Companion Activity Sheet (page 162). Then, have the student read/listen to the story. For more options, see *How To Use This Book* on page ii.

Well, I wasn't very wide awake when it happened, but I'll tell you the best that I can

remember. We were on our way home from work, singing *Hi Ho, Hi Ho*, when suddenly,

Doc _____. In the forest, we saw a pretty, young girl who _____
  (irregular past tense verb)   (irregular past tense verb)

when she saw us. We said, "Don't be afraid. You can stay with us." So, she did. She

_____ and she _____, and we loved having her around. Then
(irregular past tense verb)   (irregular past tense verb)

one day, a Witch gave her an apple. She _____ it and fell into a deep sleep. I
                                              (irregular past tense verb)

love to sleep, so I didn't think it was a big deal, but Grumpy wasn't very happy about it. He

_____ all day and night. Then, a handsome Prince came by and
  (irregular past tense verb)

_____ . Snow White woke up! They got married and _____
(irregular past tense verb)   (irregular past tense verb)

happily ever after. I slept through the whole wedding, but Happy told me all about it later.

Questions: (Answer in a complete sentence.)

❏ 1. What did Doc do when he first saw Snow White?

❏ 2. What did Snow White do when she first saw the Dwarfs?

❏ 3. What happened when Snow White ate the apple?

❏ 4. What did the handsome Prince do that woke up Snow White?

❏ 5. What did Snow White and her Prince do happily ever after?

Homework: Take a copy of this story and word/picture list home, and follow the directions above.

_____   _____   _____
Name   Homework Partner   Date

| Irregular Past Tense Verbs |

Irregular Past Tense Verbs Companion Activity Sheet

Directions: During or following the story, have the student write words from the word or picture list on the lines below. Then, have the student write sentences with these words in them.

Example: _____ *wrote* _____

*He **wrote** a letter to his friend in Japan.*

1. _____

_____

2. _____

_____

3. _____

_____

4. _____

_____

5. _____

_____

6. _____

_____

7. _____

_____

8. _____

_____

Homework: ❑ Take a copy of this sheet home with a word/picture list. Then, follow the directions above.

_____ _____ _____   **Irregular Past Tense Verbs**
Name   Homework Partner   Date

#BK-309 Grammar Tickle Stories™ • ©2004 Super Duper® Publications • 1-800-277-8737 • Online! www.superduperinc.com

A Swing and a... Hit!

Directions: Read the irregular past tense verbs on each baseball. Read each sentence on the bat and decide which irregular past tense verb is missing. Write the correct answers on the lines provided.

The batter_____at the ball and missed.

sat

The bird watchers_____around the campfire.

built

The workers_____the new mall.

bought

The Scout Troop_____cookies.

swung

The man_____the cookies.

slept

The princess_____all day and all night.

sold

Sleepy_____the story.

told

Homework: ❏ Say each irregular past tense verb in your own sentence.

❏ _____.

_____   _____   _____
Name   Homework Partner   Date

Irregular Past Tense Verbs

Irregular Past Tense Verbs

Tell your homework partner in a complete sentence:

1. Tell what you ate for breakfast.
2. Tell when you ate breakfast.

(Bonus Activity: Blow a kiss, and then tell what you just did.)

_____ _____
Name   Date

Irregular Past Tense Verbs

Tell your homework partner in a complete sentence:

1. Tell what you ate for lunch.
2. Tell where you ate lunch.

(Bonus Activity: Stick out your tongue, and then tell what you did.)

_____ _____
Name   Date

Irregular Past Tense Verbs

Tell your homework partner in a complete sentence:

1. Tell something you hung up today.
2. Tell where you hung something up today.

(Bonus Activity: Take a drink of water, and then tell what you just did.)

_____ _____
Name   Date

Irregular Past Tense Verbs

Tell your homework partner in a complete sentence:

1. Tell what you wore today.
2. Tell where you wore something today.

(Bonus Activity: Sing a few notes, and then tell what you just did.)

_____ _____
Name   Date

Irregular Past Tense Verbs

#BK-309 Grammar Tickle Stories™ • ©2004 Super Duper® Publications • 1-800-277-8737 • Online! www.superduperinc.com

Irregular Past Tense Verbs

Tell your homework partner in a complete sentence:

1. Tell what you did first when you made your bed.

2. Tell what you did second when you made your bed.

(*Bonus Activity: Write your name on a piece of paper, and then tell what you just did.*)

_____ Date

_____ Name

Irregular Past Tense Verbs

Tell your homework partner in a complete sentence:

1. Tell about something you put in your backpack.

2. Tell where you wore your backpack.

(*Bonus Activity: Give your helper a handshake, and tell what you just did.*)

_____ Date

_____ Name

Irregular Past Tense Verbs

Tell your homework partner in a complete sentence:

1. Tell about something you found this week.

2. Tell where you found something this week.

(*Bonus Activity: Pretend to hit a baseball, and tell what you just did.*)

_____ Date

_____ Name

Irregular Past Tense Verbs

Tell your homework partner in a complete sentence:

1. Tell about something you forgot this week.

2. Tell why you forgot something this week.

(*Bonus Activity: Spin around, and tell what you just did.*)

_____ Date

_____ Name

Irregular Past Tense Verbs

Supersticious Alouicious

Directions: Give each student a list of the Picture Words on pages 144 and 155 or the Word Lists on pages 145 and 156. Do not reveal the story title. Ask each student for "words" from his/her page to fill in the spaces in the story below. Write the words in the spaces. You may also have the student write these words on his/her Companion Activity Sheet (page 171). Then, have the student read/listen to the story. For more options, see *How To Use This Book* on page ii.

Alouicious was a friend of mine. He was the most superstitious person I ever knew. He

believed that if you _____ under a ladder, something bad would happen. So, he
(regular past tense verb)

always _____ while walking around ladders. He usually _____
(irregular past tense verb)   (irregular past tense verb)

down trying to do it! He heard that if a black cat _____ in front of your car, it
(irregular past tense verb)

was bad luck. He had a black cat and trained it so that it never _____ in front of
(regular past tense verb)

a car. When Alouicious spilled salt, he _____. Once, he _____ a
(regular past tense verb)   (regular past tense verb)

mirror and cut his finger. He thought that was bad luck. Whenever he counted, Alouicious

always _____ the number 13. He had 12 brothers and sisters! He always had
(irregular past tense verb)

someone to play with. I thought that made Alouicious the luckiest person I knew!

Questions: (Answer in a complete sentence)

❏ 1. What was Alouicious' superstition about ladders?

❏ 2. What did Alouicious train his cat to do?

❏ 3. What did Alouicious do when he spilled salt?

❏ 4. What did Alouicious do when he broke a mirror?

❏ 5. What did Alouicious do when he counted?

Homework: Take a copy of this story and word/picture list home, and follow the directions above.

_____   _____   _____
Name   Homework Partner   Date

**Past Tense
Verbs Combo**

#BK-309 Grammar Tickle Stories™ • ©2004 Super Duper® Publications • 1-800-277-8737 • Online! www.superduperinc.com

How I Caught A Fish

Directions: Give each student a list of the Picture Words on pages 144 and 155 or the Word Lists on pages 145 and 156. Do not reveal the story title. Ask the student for "words" from his/her page to fill in the spaces in the story below. Write the words in the spaces. You may also have the student write these words on his/her Companion Activity Sheet (page 171). Then, have the student read/listen to the story. For more options, see *How To Use This Book* on page ii.

Grandpa and I went fishing yesterday! I had never been before, so I was very

excited. He taught me how to put the worm on the hook. At first, I _____
(regular past tense verb)

because the worm was squirmy and icky. I didn't want to touch it. Then, Grandpa

_____, and I saw how easy it was. Right after that, I _____
(irregular past tense verb)   (irregular past tense verb)

and put it right on the hook. Next, Grandpa showed me how to cast the line into the

water. I watched him as he _____ his arm just the right way. He
(regular past tense verb)

_____ the line and made it look so easy. I _____ my arm,
(regular past tense verb)   (irregular past tense verb)

and before I knew it, a fish _____! "Grandpa," I yelled, "a fish bit my line!"
(regular past tense verb)

Grandpa was very proud of me. He _____, although he didn't know that I
(irregular past tense verb)

saw him. Now that's a good fish story!

Questions: (Answer in a complete sentence.)

- ❏ 1. What did the writer say he did at first because the worm was squirmy?
- ❏ 2. What did Grandpa do with the worm that made it look easy?
- ❏ 3. What did Grandpa do with his arm when he cast the line into the lake?
- ❏ 4. What did the fish do?
- ❏ 5. What did Grandpa do because he was proud?

Homework: Take a copy of this story and word/picture list home, and follow the directions above.

_____ _____ _____
Name   Homework Partner   Date

Past Tense Verbs Combo

Humph. . .

Directions: Give each student a list of the Picture Words on pages 144 and 155 or the Word Lists on pages 145 and 156. Do not reveal the story title. Ask the student for "words" from his/her page to fill in the spaces in the story below. Write the words in the spaces. You may also have the student write these words on his/her Companion Activity Sheet (Page 171). Then, have the student read/listen to the story. For more options, see *How To Use This Book* on page ii.

This is a story about camels. It is (mostly) true! Did you know that camels

_____ two million years ago! Camels _____ the earth from
(irregular past tense verb)   (regular past tense verb)

Alaska to Asia. Camels have been used for many years for travel. Even soldiers used

them. Camels _____ when the soldiers needed to go long distances.
(regular past tense verb)

Since camels _____ water in their humps, they could go for days without
(irregular past tense verb)

drinking. They often stopped and _____. When railroads were introduced,
(regular past tense verb)

they _____ faster than camels, so the camels were not needed as much
(irregular past tense verb)

for traveling. Camels have been used in the deserts of Egypt by wanderers called

Nomads. The Nomads _____ all year, so they needed camels to carry
(irregular past tense verb)

their goods. At the zoo, camels have _____ for grownups and children
(regular past tense verb)

alike. Don't get to close to a camel because one slobbered on me. "Humph!" I said.

Questions: (Answer in a complete sentence.)

❏ 1. What did the camels do two million years ago?

❏ 2. What did camels do when the soldiers needed to go long distances?

❏ 3. What did the camels often stop and do?

❏ 4. What did the Nomads do all year?

❏ 5. What have camels done at the zoo?

Homework: Take a copy of this story and word/picture list home, and follow the directions above.

_____   _____   _____
Name   Homework Partner   Date

Past Tense Verbs Combo

#BK-309 Grammar Tickle Stories™ • ©2004 Super Duper® Publications • 1-800-277-8737 • Online! www.superduperinc.com

Appetite For Fun

Directions: Give each student a list of the Picture Words on pages 144 and 155 or the Word Lists on pages 145 and 156. Do not reveal the story title. Ask the student for "words" from his/her page to fill in the spaces in the story below. Write the words in the spaces. You may also have the student write these words on his/her Companion Activity Sheet (page 171). Then, have the student read/listen to the story. For more options, see *How To Use This Book* on page ii.

"FUN"- RAISER

This year we're going to have a pancake breakfast to raise money for the new school

auditorium. Last year's breakfast was such a success that we are going to do it again! If

you remember our principal, Mr. Schooly, _____ those pancakes until they

(regular past tense verb)

were golden brown! He flipped them into the air, and they _____ right on the

(irregular past tense verb)

plate! Everyone yelled, "Yea" and _____. Mr. Schooly turned bright red and

(regular past tense verb)

_____, but we knew he was happy. Mrs. Stickybuns was in charge of the

(regular past tense verb)

syrup, which she _____ so well that we're going to let her do it again. When

(irregular past tense verb)

the breakfast was over, our PE teacher, Mr. Laps, had ball drills. The students

_____ and _____. We all had a ball! So, come sign up! You'll

(irregular past tense verb)   (regular past tense verb)

want to be able to tell your friends you _____ at the pancake breakfast!

(irregular past tense verb)

Questions: (Answer in a complete sentence.)

❏ 1. What did Mr. Schooly do last year until the pancakes were golden brown?

❏ 2. What did Mr. Schooly do after he turned bright red?

❏ 3. What did Mrs. Stickybuns do with the syrup?

❏ 4. What did the students do with the balls Mr. Laps brought out?

❏ 5. What do you want to be able to tell your friends that you did at the pancake breakfast?

Homework: Take a copy of this story and word/picture list home, and follow the directions above.

_____ _____ _____

Name   Homework Partner   Date

Past Tense Verbs Combo

And The Band Played On. . .

Directions: Give each student a list of the Picture Words on pages 144 and 155 or the Word Lists on pages 145 and 156. Do not reveal the story title. Ask the student for "words" from his/her page to fill in the spaces in the story below. Write the words in the spaces. You may also have the student write these words on his/her Companion Activity Sheet (page 171). Then, have the student read/listen to the story. For more options, see *How To Use This Book* on page ii.

Yesterday the Mayor came to our town. Everyone was excited. The towns people

had prepared for weeks. The marching band _____ down the street and
_____(regular past tense verb)_____

the baton twirlers _____ their batons in rhythm to the band. It was so
_____(regular past tense verb)_____

exciting that some people _____! The firefighters put on quite a show!
_____(irregular past tense verb)_____

They _____ their fire trucks and _____ their horns as they
_____(irregular past tense verb)_____   _____(regular past tense verb)_____

drove by. We even had clowns who _____ just for the mayor! Later,
_____(irregular past tense verb)_____

the Mayor said, "I was so excited that I _____." The Mayor's wife
_____(regular past tense verb)_____

_____ because she was the happiest person there. That was one great
(irregular past tense verb)

parade!

Questions: (Answer in a complete sentence.)

❏ 1. What did the marching band do?

❏ 2. What did the baton twirlers do in rhythm with the band?

❏ 3. What did the firefighters do with their trucks and their horns?

❏ 4. What did the clowns do?

❏ 5. What did the mayor say he did and what did the mayor's wife do?

Homework: Take a copy of this story and word/picture list home, and follow the directions above.

_____   _____   _____
Name   Homework Partner   Date

Past Tense Verbs Combo

#BK-309 Grammar Tickle Stories™ • ©2004 Super Duper® Publications • 1-800-277-8737 • Online! www.superduperinc.com

Past Tense Verbs Combo Companion Activity Sheet

Directions: During or following the story, have the student write words from the word or picture list on the lines below. Then, have the student write sentences with these words in them.

Example: _____ ***clapped*** _____   - OR -   _____ ***drew*** _____

*The fans **clapped** after the team scored a touchdown.*   *The girl **drew** a picture.*

1. _____

_____

2. _____

_____

3. _____

_____

4. _____

_____

5. _____

_____

6. _____

_____

7. _____

_____

8. _____

_____

Homework: ❑ Take a copy of this sheet home with a word/picture list. Then, follow the directions above.

_____   _____   _____

Name   Homework Partner   Date

Past Tense Verbs Combo

Fishing For The Right Word!

Directions: Read the sentences and circle the word in the fish that uses the correct regular or irregular past tense verb form to complete the sentence. _____

1. Grandpa  catched/caught a fish.

2. Mr. Schooly  blushed/blush when he flipped the pancakes.

3. The camel  carry/carried the packs across the desert.

4. The boy 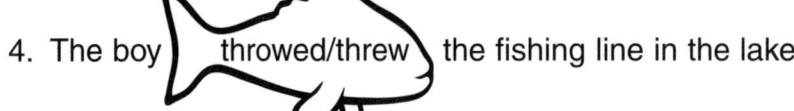 throwed/threw the fishing line in the lake.

5. Alouicious  walk/walked around the ladder.

6. The camel  drank/drinked the water from the watering hole.

Homework: ❑ Say each past tense verb in your own sentence.

❑ _____ .

| Name | Homework Partner | Date | **Past Tense Verbs Combo** |

#BK-309 Grammar Tickle Stories™ • ©2004 Super Duper® Publications • 1-800-277-8737 • Online! www.superduperinc.com

Past Tense Verbs Combo

Fill in the sentences with a correct past tense verb form in the spaces provided. Answer in complete sentences.

1. I _____ the ball to my friend.

2. My friend _____ the ball that I threw.

Name _____

Date _____

Past Tense Verbs Combo

Fill in the sentences with a correct past tense verb form in the spaces provided. Answer in complete sentences.

1. I _____ my friend on the phone.

2. My friend _____ the phone when I called.

Name _____

Date _____

Past Tense Verbs Combo

Fill in the sentences with a correct past tense verb form in the spaces provided. Answer in complete sentences.

1. The band _____ music all night.

2. When they were done, I _____ them that I liked their music.

Name _____

Date _____

Past Tense Verbs Combo

Fill in the sentences with a correct past tense verb form in the spaces provided. Answer in complete sentences.

1. I went fishing, and this is the fish that I _____!

2. My Grandpa's fishing line got tangled in some seaweed, so he _____ it with scissors.

Name _____

Date _____

Past Tense Verbs Combo

Past Tense Verbs Combo

Fill in the sentence with a correct past tense verb form in the spaces provided. Answer in a complete sentece.

1. In old days, Nomads _____ on their camels across the desert.

2. When they came to a watering hole, the camels _____ water and stored it in their humps.

_____   _____
Name   Date

Past Tense Verbs Combo

Fill in the sentence with a correct past tense verb form in the spaces provided. Answer in a complete sentece.

1. I didn't believe that if you _____ under a ladder it was bad luck.

2. I tripped and _____ under a ladder, so now I walk around it!

_____   _____
Name   Date

Past Tense Verbs Combo

Fill in the sentence with a correct past tense verb form in the spaces provided. Answer in a complete sentece.

1. Our music chorus _____ many songs at the concert last night.

2. We were so good that we _____ first place.

_____   _____
Name   Date

Past Tense Verbs Combo

Fill in the sentence with a correct past tense verb form in the spaces provided. Answer in a complete sentece.

1. Yesterday our teacher _____ us to write a letter to someone special.

2. I _____ my letter to my Uncle Frank who lives on a farm.

_____   _____
Name   Date

Past Tense Verbs Combo

Future Tense Verbs

Future Tense

Directions: Use the picture words below to help you complete the stories on pages 178 to 182.

will catch

will eat

will pour

will sleep

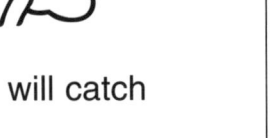

will cry

will fall

will read

will swim

will dance

will jump

will ride

will swing

will draw

will laugh

will run

will throw

will drink

will open

will sing

will walk

will drive

will paint

will skateboard

will write

Future Tense Verbs

#BK-309 Grammar Tickle Stories™ • ©2004 Super Duper® Publications • 1-800-277-8737 • Online! www.superduperinc.com

Future Tense Verbs

Directions: Use these words to help complete the stories on pages 178 to 182.

- ❏ will act
- ❏ will bake
- ❏ will bark
- ❏ will bathe
- ❏ will bend
- ❏ will blow
- ❏ will break
- ❏ will brush
- ❏ will build
- ❏ will call
- ❏ will carry
- ❏ will catch
- ❏ will chase
- ❏ will chew
- ❏ will choose
- ❏ will clap
- ❏ will clean
- ❏ will climb
- ❏ will close
- ❏ will color
- ❏ will comb
- ❏ will cough
- ❏ will crawl
- ❏ will cry
- ❏ will cut
- ❏ will dance
- ❏ will draw
- ❏ will dream
- ❏ will dress
- ❏ will drink
- ❏ will drive
- ❏ will eat
- ❏ will fall
- ❏ will feed
- ❏ will fix
- ❏ will fly

- ❏ will fold
- ❏ will give
- ❏ will help
- ❏ will hide
- ❏ will hold
- ❏ will hop
- ❏ will hug
- ❏ will jump
- ❏ will laugh
- ❏ will listen
- ❏ will look
- ❏ will march
- ❏ will meow
- ❏ will open
- ❏ will paint
- ❏ will paste
- ❏ will pitch
- ❏ will plant
- ❏ will play
- ❏ will pour
- ❏ will pull
- ❏ will push
- ❏ will rain
- ❏ will reach
- ❏ will read
- ❏ will ride
- ❏ will ring
- ❏ will roll
- ❏ will row
- ❏ will run
- ❏ will sew
- ❏ will share
- ❏ will shop
- ❏ will sing
- ❏ will skateboard
- ❏ will ski

- ❏ will sleep
- ❏ will slide
- ❏ will smile
- ❏ will snow
- ❏ will spend
- ❏ will spill
- ❏ will splash
- ❏ will study
- ❏ will surf
- ❏ will surprise
- ❏ will sweep
- ❏ will swim
- ❏ will swing
- ❏ will taste
- ❏ will teach
- ❏ will tear
- ❏ will throw
- ❏ will tickle
- ❏ will twist
- ❏ will walk
- ❏ will wash
- ❏ will watch
- ❏ will wave
- ❏ will work
- ❏ will wrap
- ❏ will write
- ❏ will yawn
- ❏ will yell
- ❏ will zip

Future Tense Verbs

Tennis Anyone!

Directions: Give each student a list of the Picture Words on page 176 or the Word List on page 177. Do not reveal the story title. Ask the student for "words" from his/her page to fill in the spaces in the story below. Write the words in the spaces. You may also have the student write these words on his/her Companion Activity Sheet (page 183). Then, have the student read/listen to the story. For more options, see *How To Use This Book* on page ii.

Advertisement

Tennis is fast becoming a very popular sport. If you want to get in on this growing

phenomenon, take advantage of this special offer. If you sign up today, here is what you

can expect. On your first day, you _____! Believe it or not, you
　　　　　　　　　　　　　　　　　　　　　　(future tense verb)

_____ on your very first visit! In Lesson Two, you'll learn to improve your
(future tense verb)

swing. The instructor _____. You can watch until you think you're ready to
　　　　　　　　　　　　(future tense verb)

try it on your own. By the Fifth Lesson, you _____ with the best of them.
　　　　　　　　　　　　　　　　　　　　　　　(future tense verb)

Then, it will be time to try out your new skills on the court. First, you

_____ and your partner _____. By then, you should be
(future tense verb)　　　　　　　　　　　(future tense verb)

comfortable swinging the racket. The hardest part is the serve. No doubt you

_____. The crowd will go wild, and I'll bet that they _____.
(future tense verb)　　　　　　　　　　　　　　　　　　　　　　　　　　(future tense verb)

So, tennis anyone?

Questions: (Answer in a complete sentence.)

❏ 1. What does the ad say you will do on your first day?

❏ 2. What does the ad say the instructor will do?

❏ 3. What does the ad say you'll do by the fifth lesson?

❏ 4. What does the ad say your partner will do on the court?

❏ 5. What does the ad "bet" that the crowd will do?

Homework: Take a copy of this story and word/picture list home, and follow the directions above.

_____　　_____　　_____
Name　　　　　　　　　　Homework Partner　　　　　　　Date

Future Tense Verbs

Future Superheroes Toys

Directions: Give each student a list of the Picture Words on page 176 or the Word List on page 177. Do not reveal the story title. Ask the student for "words" from his/her page to fill in the spaces in the story below. Write the words in the spaces. You may also have the student write these words on his/her Companion Activity Sheet (page 183). Then, have the student read/listen to the story. For more options, see *How To Use This Book* on page ii.

Can you imagine what a future superhero toy might be like? I think they

_____! It's possible that they will build wings on them so they
(future tense verb)

_____. Maybe they will make them with rollers on their feet and they
(future tense verb)

_____. They could change an older superhero, or perhaps invent a new
(future tense verb)

one. Either way, they _____ off the shelves at the store. When asked to
(future tense verb)

guess what the new superheroes will be able to do, one boy said, "I think they

_____." The little girl next to him said, "No, they _____."
(future tense verb)   (future tense verb)

When these same two children were asked what superheroes will do in the future, he

said, "I think they _____." She answered, "I think they _____."
(future tense verb)   (future tense verb)

That's Super!

Questions: (Answer in a complete sentence.)

❏ 1. What does the writer think future superheroes will do with wings?

❏ 2. What does the writer think future superheroes will do with rollers on their feet?

❏ 3. What did the boy think they will do?

❏ 4. What did the little girl think they will do?

❏ 5. What will the little boy and girl do someday?

Homework: Take a copy of this story and word/picture list home, and follow the directions above.

_____   _____   _____

Name   Homework Partner   Date

Future Tense Verbs

Costumes by Design

Directions: Give each student a list of the Picture Words on page 176 or the Word List on page 177. Do not reveal the story title. Ask the student for "words" from his/her page to fill in the spaces in the story below. Write the words in the spaces. You may also have the student write these words on his/her Companion Activity Sheet (page 183). Then, have the student read/listen to the story. For more options, see *How To Use This Book* on page ii.

Announcing: The Costume Contest

This year we will hold our annual *Costume Contest* in October. If you want to enter,

this is what you'll need to do. First, you _____. Then, you can pick up
(future tense verb)

your contest form. You _____ and take this form home. Your parents
(future tense verb)

_____, and you can talk about your good ideas. Next, you
(future tense verb)

_____ and decide on what materials you will need to gather. I am sure
(future tense verb)

you _____, while you think about what you want to make. After you are
(future tense verb)

done, you _____ and bring them to school on the last day. The judges
(future tense verb)

_____, as you walk around wearing your costumes. The other students
(future tense verb)

_____. Then, the judges will announce the names of the winners.
(future tense verb)

Good luck!

Questions: (Answer in a complete sentence.)

❑ 1. What will you do first?

❑ 2. What will your parents do?

❑ 3. What will you do after you are done?

❑ 4. What will the judges do as you parade around wearing your costume?

❑ 5. What will the other students do?

Homework: Take a copy of this story and word/picture list home, and follow the directions above.

_____   _____   _____
Name   Homework Partner   Date

Future Tense Verbs

#BK-309 Grammar Tickle Stories™ • ©2004 Super Duper® Publications • 1-800-277-8737 • Online! www.superduperinc.com

Trip to the Lake

Directions: Give each student a list of the Picture Words on page 176 or the Word List on page 177. Do not reveal the story title. Ask the student for "words" from his/her page to fill in the spaces in the story below. Write the words in the spaces. You may also have the student write these words on his/her Companion Activity Sheet (page 183). Then, have the student read/listen to the story. For more options, see *How To Use This Book* on page ii.

Last night our family talked about going to the lake! My mom said, "The sun

_____!" I asked my dad if we could take the boat, and he said, "The boat
(future tense verb)

_____!" I asked what we would do there. My brother said, "We
(future tense verb)

_____." I wondered if ants would ruin our picnic. My uncle said, "The
(future tense verb)

ants _____ when they see us!" I also wanted to know if we could take our
(future tense verb)

puppy Scooter. My dad said, "Scooter _____ if we take him, so we'll
(future tense verb)

leave him with friends." My mom said, "Just think, when we get home, Scooter

_____ with excitement." "Will we bring him a present?" I asked my mom.
(future tense verb)

Mom said, "Yes, we _____ every chance we get." I wanted to know if we
(future tense verb)

would have a good time. Everyone said, "We _____ until the cows come
(future tense verb)

home!" Now that sounds like fun!

Questions: (Answer in a complete sentence.)

❑ 1. What does Mom say the sun will do?

❑ 2. What does the brother say they will do there?

❑ 3. What does the uncle say the ants will do?

❑ 4. What will Scooter do if they take him?

❑ 5. What will they do "til the cows come home?"

Homework: Take a copy of this story and word/picture list home, and follow the directions above.

_____   _____   _____

Name   Homework Partner   Date

Future Tense Verbs

What Will Be Will Be

Directions: Give each student a list of the Picture Words on page 176 or the Word List on page 177. Do not reveal the story title. Ask the student for "words" from his/her page to fill in the spaces in the story below. Write the words in the spaces. You may also have the student write these words on his/her Companion Activity Sheet (page 183). Then, have the student read/listen to the story. For more options, see *How To Use This Book* on page ii.

Imagine what the future will be like. I think that, with the kind of cars we'll be driving,

we _____ right off the roads and into the skies! People
　　(future tense verb)

_____ like they've never done before. Our televisions _____
　(future tense verb)　　　　　　　　　　　　　　　　　　　　　　　(future tense verb)

and our computers _____. It's exciting to think about, isn't it? Home
　　　　　　　　(future tense verb)

robots will see to your every need. If you want your room cleaned, your personal robot

_____. If you need help with your homework, your robot
　(future tense verb)

_____ and help you out. Teachers of the future will have to learn new
　(future tense verb)

things, so that they can teach their students. Teachers _____ in the world
　　　　　　　　　　　　　　　　　　　　　　　　(future tense verb)

of tomorrow. What will you do in the future? Just close your eyes and say, "Tomorrow, I

_____." It just might not be that far off!
　(future tense verb)

Questions: (Answer in a complete sentence.)
- ❏ 1. What will we do in the cars of the future?
- ❏ 2. What will people do like never before?
- ❏ 3. What will your personal robot do?
- ❏ 4. What will teachers of the future need to learn to do?
- ❏ 5. What should you close your eyes and say?

Homework: Take a copy of this story and word/picture list home, and follow the directions above.

_____　　_____　　_____
　　　　Name　　　　　　　　Homework Partner　　　　　　　Date

| Future Tense Verbs |

#BK-309 Grammar Tickle Stories™ • ©2004 Super Duper® Publications • 1-800-277-8737 • Online! www.superduperinc.com

Future Tense Verbs Companion Activity Sheet

Directions: During or following the story, have the student write words from the word or picture list on the lines below. Then, have the student write sentences with these words in them.

Example: _____ ***will cry*** _____

*The baby **will cry** when he gets hungry.*

1. _____

_____

2. _____

_____

3. _____

_____

4. _____

_____

5. _____

_____

6. _____

_____

7. _____

_____

8. _____

_____

Homework: ❏ Take a copy of this sheet home with a word/picture list. Then, follow the directions above.

_____ _____ _____ | Future Tense Verbs |
Name | Homework Partner | Date

Where There's A Will...

Directions: Write the letters **a** through **f** on small cards. Have the students roll a die and read the sentence that corresponds to the number on the die. Then, have the student choose a letter card and read the corresponding answer. Enjoy the silly sentences! If a correct match is made, score a point! <u>Game option</u>: Make a check each time you use a number and letter. The first person to check off all their numbers and letters wins!

1. The first time you play tennis you...   a. ...will hit the ball with the racket.

2. In the future, superheroes...   b. ...will save the world.

3. Your next costume...   c. ...will be ready in time for the contest.

4. At the costume contest, the judges...   d. ...will choose a winner.

5. When we go to the lake, the sun...   e. ...will shine!

6. In the future, cars...   f. ...will fly.

Homework: ❏ Take a copy of this sheet home with a word/picture list. Then, follow the directions above

❏ _____..

_____   _____   _____

Name   Homework Partner   Date

Future Tense Verbs

#BK-309 Grammar Tickle Stories™ • ©2004 Super Duper® Publications • 1-800-277-8737 • Online! www.superduperinc.com

Future Tense Verbs

Tell your homework partner in a complete sentence:

1. Tell what you will do for homework.

2. Tell when you will do your homework.

(Bonus Activity: What will you do after you do homework?)

Name _____

Date _____

Future Tense Verbs

Tell your homework partner in a complete sentence:

1. Tell what you will do to clean your room.

2. Tell why you will clean your room.

(Bonus Activity: What will you do after you clean your room?)

Name _____

Date _____

Future Tense Verbs

Tell your homework partner in a complete sentence:

1. Tell what you will eat for dinner.

2. Tell when you will eat dinner.

(Bonus Activity: What will you do after you eat dinner?)

Name _____

Date _____

Future Tense Verbs

Tell your homework partner in a complete sentence:

1. Tell what you will do on Saturday.

2. Tell why you will do it on Saturday.

(Bonus Activity: What will you do on Sunday?)

Name _____

Date _____

Future Tense Verbs

Future Tense Verbs

Tell your homework partner in a complete sentence:

1. Tell what you will do to help with the chores at home.

2. Tell why you will help with the chores at home.

(Bonus Activity: What will you do after you do your chores?)

_____ _____
Name   Date

Future Tense Verbs

Tell your homework partner in a complete sentence:

1. Tell when you will brush your teeth.

2. Tell why you will brush your teeth.

(Bonus Activity: What will you do after you brush your teeth?)

_____ _____
Name   Date

Future Tense Verbs

Tell your homework partner in a complete sentence:

1. Tell what you will do at school tomorrow.

2. Tell what you will do when you first get to school tomorrow.

(Bonus Activity: What will you do when you get home from school tomorrow?)

_____ _____
Name   Date

Future Tense Verbs

Tell your homework partner in a complete sentence:

1. Tell when you will have your next birthday.

2. Tell what you will do for your next birthday.

(Bonus Activity: Where will you have your next birthday?)

_____ _____
Name   Date

Future Tense Verbs

#BK-309 Grammar Tickle Stories™ • ©2004 Super Duper® Publications • 1-800-277-8737 • Online! www.superduperinc.com

Subject/Verb Agreement

Singular and Plural

Subject/Verb Agreement Singular

Directions: Use the picture words below to help you complete the stories on pages 190 to 194 and 210 to 214.

catches

eats

pours

sleeps

cries

falls

reads

swims

dances

jumps

rides

swings

draws

laughs

runs

throws

drinks

opens

sings

walks

drives

paints

skateboards

writes

#BK-309 Grammar Tickle Stories™ • ©2004 Super Duper® Publications • 1-800-277-8737 • Online! www.superduperinc.com

Subject/Verb Agreement Singular

Directions: Use these words to help complete the stories on pages 190 to 194.

- ❏ acts
- ❏ bakes
- ❏ barks
- ❏ bathes
- ❏ bends
- ❏ blows
- ❏ breaks
- ❏ brushes
- ❏ builds
- ❏ calls
- ❏ carries
- ❏ catches
- ❏ chases
- ❏ chews
- ❏ chooses
- ❏ claps
- ❏ cleans
- ❏ climbs
- ❏ closes
- ❏ colors
- ❏ combs
- ❏ coughs
- ❏ crawls
- ❏ cries
- ❏ cuts
- ❏ dances
- ❏ draws
- ❏ dreams
- ❏ dresses
- ❏ drinks
- ❏ drives
- ❏ eats
- ❏ falls
- ❏ feeds
- ❏ fixes
- ❏ flies
- ❏ folds
- ❏ gives

- ❏ helps
- ❏ hides
- ❏ holds
- ❏ hops
- ❏ hugs
- ❏ jumps
- ❏ laughs
- ❏ listens
- ❏ looks
- ❏ marches
- ❏ meows
- ❏ opens
- ❏ paints
- ❏ pastes
- ❏ pitches
- ❏ plants
- ❏ plays
- ❏ pours
- ❏ pulls
- ❏ pushes
- ❏ rains
- ❏ reaches
- ❏ reads
- ❏ rides
- ❏ rings
- ❏ rolls
- ❏ rows
- ❏ runs
- ❏ sews
- ❏ shares
- ❏ shops
- ❏ sings
- ❏ skateboards
- ❏ sleeps

- ❏ slides
- ❏ smiles
- ❏ snows
- ❏ spends
- ❏ spills
- ❏ splashes
- ❏ studies
- ❏ surfs
- ❏ surprises
- ❏ sweeps
- ❏ swims
- ❏ swings
- ❏ tastes
- ❏ teaches
- ❏ tears
- ❏ throws
- ❏ tickles
- ❏ twists
- ❏ walks
- ❏ washes
- ❏ watches
- ❏ waves
- ❏ works
- ❏ wraps
- ❏ writes
- ❏ yawns
- ❏ yells
- ❏ zips

Subject / Verb Agreement Singular

Why You Should Buy This Dog

Directions: Give each student a list of the Picture Words on page 188 or the Word List on page 189. Do not reveal the story title. Ask the student for "words" from his/her page to fill in the spaces in the story below. Write the words in the spaces. You may also have the student write these words on his/her Companion Activity Sheet (page 195). Then, have the student read/listen to the story. For more options, see *How To Use This Book* on page ii.

DOG OF THE WEEK AD: CASEY

Look at this adorable picture! The person who _____ this picture will
(subject/verb singular)

not be able to resist Casey! We first fell in love with how she _____ when
(subject/verb singular)

she greets us. When she's very excited, she _____, but when she's tired,
(subject/verb singular)

she just lays there and _____. When she sees the other dogs, she
(subject/verb singular)

immediately _____ and wants to play. Everyone here wants to take her
(subject/verb singular)

home! We guarantee you'll fall in love with the way she _____. Dr. Digger,
(subject/verb singular)

our local veterinarian said, "Casey is so smart. When you ask her, she

_____ and rolls over. She is so loveable." So, come down today and see
(subject/verb singular)

for yourself. If she _____ when she sees you, you'll know that she's the
(subject/verb singular)

dog for you!

Questions: (Answer in a complete sentence.)

- ❏ 1. According to this ad, what does Casey do when she greets us?
- ❏ 2. What does Casey do when she's very excited?
- ❏ 3. What does Casey do when she's tired?
- ❏ 4. What does Casey do when she sees other dogs?
- ❏ 5. What does Dr. Digger say Casey does when you ask her to?

Homework: Take a copy of this story and word/picture list home, and follow the directions above.

_____   _____   _____

Name   Homework Partner   Date

#BK-309 Grammar Tickle Stories™ • ©2004 Super Duper® Publications • 1-800-277-8737 • Online! www.superduperinc.com

Learn to Juggle Video

Directions: Give each student a list of the Picture Words on page 188 or the Word List on page 189. Do not reveal the story title. Ask the student for "words" from his/her page to fill in the spaces in the story below. Write the words in the spaces. You may also have the student write these words on his/her Companion Activity Sheet (page 195). Then, have the student read/listen to the story. For more options, see *How To Use This Book* on page ii.

With the help of my Junior Jugglers, Billy and Charlene, I'm going to teach you how

to juggle. You'll need three round objects. Notice how easily Billy _____
(subject/verb singular)

that rubber ball in the air. Charlene _____ her orange. Of course, ask
(subject/verb singular)

your parents before using fruit because it _____ if you drop it! First, we'll
(subject/verb singular)

do some exercises to warm up your hands. Watch Billy. His left hand

_____, while his right hand _____. It's easier than it looks!
(subject/verb singular)   (subject/verb singular)

It's important to keep your eyes on whatever you're juggling. Watch Charlene. Her left

eye _____ and her right eye _____. Try it! Now we're going
(subject/verb singular)   (subject/verb singular)

to get ready to juggle, so take your objects and let's begin. Soon you'll be so excited,

you'll call out, "Juggling _____!"
(subject/verb singular)

Questions: (Answer in a complete sentence.)

- ❏ 1. What does Billy do with the rubber ball?
- ❏ 2. What does Charlene do with her orange?
- ❏ 3. What does fruit do when you drop it?
- ❏ 4. What does Billy's left hand do? What does his right hand do?
- ❏ 5. What will you soon yell excitedly about juggling?

Homework: Take a copy of this story and word/picture list home, and follow the directions above.

_____   _____   _____
Name   Homework Partner   Date

Subject / Verb Agreement Singular

Dog Training Class

Directions: Give each student a list of the Picture Words on page 188 or the Word List on page 189. Do not reveal the story title. Ask the student for "words" from his/her page to fill in the spaces in the story below. Write the words in the spaces. You may also have the student write these words on his/her Companion Activity Sheet (page 195). Then, have the student read/listen to the story. For more options, see *How To Use This Book* on page ii.

Today we will learn the basics of training your dog. My dog, Poochie, will

demonstrate. When I hold my hand up like this, Poochie _____. When I
(subject/verb singular)

put my hand down by my side, Poochie _____. Now, if you hope that your
(subject/verb singular)

dog _____ when you call it, just be patient with your pet. Poochie likes
(subject/verb singular)

treats. Watch how Poochie _____ when I hold this snack in front of him.
(subject/verb singular)

Poochie likes me to scratch his ears. So, he _____ when he wants me to
(subject/verb singular)

scratch him. If I throw a ball, Poochie _____ it. But, if I throw a stick, he
(subject/verb singular)

_____ it. Most of all, your dog just wants to know you love him. Give your
(subject/verb singular)

dog a nice pat on the head and watch how it _____! For our next class,
(subject/verb singular)

we'll learn more dog commands.

Questions: (Answer in a complete sentence.)
- ❏ 1. What does Poochie do when the trainer holds up his hand?
- ❏ 2. What does Poochie do when the trainer puts his hand down?
- ❏ 3. What does Poochie do for treats?
- ❏ 4. What does Poochie do when he wants his ears scratched?
- ❏ 5. What does Poochie do when the trainer throws a ball? a stick?

Homework: Take a copy of this story and word/picture list home, and follow the directions above.

_____ _____ _____
Name Homework Partner Date

Subject / Verb Agreement Singular

#BK-309 Grammar Tickle Stories™ • ©2004 Super Duper® Publications • 1-800-277-8737 • Online! www.superduperinc.com

Music In Review

Directions: Give each student a list of the Picture Words on page 188 or the Word List on page 189. Do not reveal the story title. Ask the student for "words" from his/her page to fill in the spaces in the story below. Write the words in the spaces. You may also have the student write these words on his/her Companion Activity Sheet (page 195). Then, have the student read/listen to the story. For more options, see *How To Use This Book* on page ii.

No doubt about it, the band, Rocks In Our Socks, _____! The drummer
(subject/verb singular)

_____ his drums loudly. The lead guitar player _____ his
(subject/verb singular)   (subject/verb singular)

guitar. The lead singer, well, she _____ a song like no one you've ever
(subject/verb singular)

heard before! Before they even come on stage, the spotlight comes on and

_____ the stage. Then, the announcer _____, and by then,
(subject/verb singular)   (subject/verb singular)

the audience is really going wild. When the band finally comes on, the audience

_____ to let the band members know how much they like them. When the
(subject/verb singular)

band members are done, the audience stands and _____ for about five
(subject/verb singular)

minutes! It's a show well worth seeing!

Questions: (Answer in a complete sentence.)

❏ 1. What does the drummer do?

❏ 2. What does the lead guitar player do?

❏ 3. What does the singer do?

❏ 4. What does the audience do to let the band know they like them?

❏ 5. What does the audience stand and do when the band is done?

Homework: Take a copy of this story and word/picture list home, and follow the directions above.

_____   _____   _____
      Name   Homework Partner   Date

Subject/Verb Agreement Singular

Designing Time

Directions: Give each student a list of the Picture Words on page 188 or the Word List on page 189. Do not reveal the story title. Ask the student for "words" from his/her page to fill in the spaces in the story below. Write the words in the spaces. You may also have the student write these words on his/her Companion Activity Sheet (page 195). Then, have the student read/listen to the story. For more options, see *How To Use This Book* on page ii.

It's time for our annual *T-shirt Design Contest* for the School Carnival. We've

prepared a fashion show with some of our past winners. Let's take a look. Here's Amy.

She is wearing a shirt that _____ in the dark! As she turns, see how it
(subject/verb singular)

_____? Next, Todd's shirt _____ when he walks, and it
(subject/verb singular)   (subject/verb singular)

_____ when he walks backwards! Here is last year's winner, Davey. He
(subject/verb singular)

_____ every time he puts that shirt on! His mom is so proud, she
(subject/verb singular)

_____ when he wears it. The only thing you need to remember about
(subject/verb singular)

designing a T-shirt is that it _____. Remember, our school motto is going
(subject/verb singular)

on the shirt: "Our School _____." Now back to your drawing boards. It's
(subject/verb singular)

design time!

Questions: (Answer in a complete sentence.)

❏ 1. What does Amy's shirt do in the dark?

❏ 2. What does Todd's shirt do when he walks?

❏ 3. What does Davey do every time he puts his shirt on?

❏ 4. What does Davey's mom do because she's so proud?

❏ 5. What does the school motto say?

Homework: Take a copy of this story and word/picture list home, and follow the directions above.

_____ _____ _____

Name   Homework Partner   Date

Subject/Verb Agreement Singular

#BK-309 Grammar Tickle Stories™ • ©2004 Super Duper® Publications • 1-800-277-8737 • Online! www.superduperinc.com

Subject/Verb Agreement Singular Companion Activity Sheet

Directions: During or following the story, have the student write words from the word or picture list on the lines below. Then, have the student write sentences with these words in them.

Example: _____**dances**_____

_____She **dances** to the music on the radio._____

1. _____

_____

2. _____

_____

3. _____

_____

4. _____

_____

5. _____

_____

6. _____

_____

7. _____

_____

8. _____

_____

Homework: ❏ Take a copy of this sheet home with a word/picture list. Then, follow the directions above.

_____ _____ _____

Name   Homework Partner   Date

What Go/Goes There?

Directions: Read the following paragraphs and decide what's wrong in each sentence. Fix it by writing (or have someone write for you) the correct form of the verb on the line.

1. Casey <u>wag</u> her tail when she's excited. _____

   She <u>sit</u> up when you ask her. _____

   The person who <u>buy</u> her is really lucky! _____

2. Billy <u>throw</u> the ball in the air. _____

   Charlene <u>catch</u> the ball. _____

   Sometimes, the ball <u>drop</u>. _____

3. Amy's shirt <u>glow</u> in the dark. _____

   Todd's shirt <u>change</u> colors when he turns. _____

   Davey is so proud every time he <u>wear</u> his t-shirt. _____

4. Poochie <u>obey</u> commands. _____

   Poochie <u>fetch</u> a stick on command. _____

   Watch out! Poochie <u>lick</u> your face when you come in! _____

5. The rock group <u>play</u> music. _____

   The drummer <u>hit</u> the drums with drumsticks. _____

   The singer <u>sing</u> with the music. _____

   The audience <u>applaud</u> if they like the song. _____

Homework: ❑ Take a copy of this sheet home with a word/picture list. Then, follow the directions above.

   ❑ _____.

_____ _____ _____
Name   Homework Partner   Date

Subject/Verb Agreement Singular

#BK-309 Grammar Tickle Stories™ • ©2004 Super Duper® Publications • 1-800-277-8737 • Online! www.superduperinc.com

Subject/Verb Agreement Singular

Fill in the sentences with the correct subject/verb agreement form. Answer in a complete sentence.

1. My dog (bury) his bone. First, he (dig) a hole and then, he (bury) it.

2. Later, when he wants to find it, he (dig) it up again.

_____
Name

_____
Date

Subject/Verb Agreement Singular

Fill in the sentences with the correct subject/verb agreement form. Answer in a complete sentence.

1. Grandma (read) to us when she comes to visit.

2. She (read) us books from when she was a little girl!

_____
Name

_____
Date

Subject/Verb Agreement Singular

Fill in the sentences with the correct subject/verb agreement form. Answer in a complete sentence.

1. Our coach (teach) us how to play baseball.

2. The batter (hit) the ball and (run) to first base.

_____
Name

_____
Date

Subject/Verb Agreement Singular

Fill in the sentences with the correct subject/verb agreement form. Answer in a complete sentence.

1. The band really (rock) when they play their music.

2. The audience (clap) and (yell) because they like the music.

_____
Name

_____
Date

Subject/Verb Agreement Singular

Subject/Verb Agreement Singular

Fill in the sentences with the correct subject/verb agreement form. Answer in a complete sentence.

1. My mom (bake) special cakes on our birthdays.

2. When she (bake), she always lets me lick the bowl!

Name _____

Date _____

Subject/Verb Agreement Singular

Fill in the sentences with the correct subject/verb agreement form. Answer in a complete sentence.

1. My parrot, Loudmouth, always (talk) to me when I come in the room.

2. My parrot (talk) to me, but I don't understand what he's saying.

Name _____

Date _____

Subject/Verb Agreement Singular

Fill in the sentences with the correct subject/verb agreement form. Answer in a complete sentence.

1. My cat (meow) when she wants me to rub her tummy.

2. When I stop, she (meow) even louder!

Name _____

Date _____

Subject/Verb Agreement Singular

Fill in the sentences with the correct subject/verb agreement form. Answer in a complete sentence.

1. When we play Hide and Seek, my little sister always (hide) in the closet.

2. I always find her because she (hide) in the same place!

Name _____

Date _____

Subject/Verb Agreement Singular

#BK-309 Grammar Tickle Stories™ • ©2004 Super Duper® Publications • 1-800-277-8737 • Online! www.superduperinc.com

Subject/Verb Agreement Plural

Directions: Use the picture words below to help you complete the stories on pages 201 to 205 and 210 to 214.

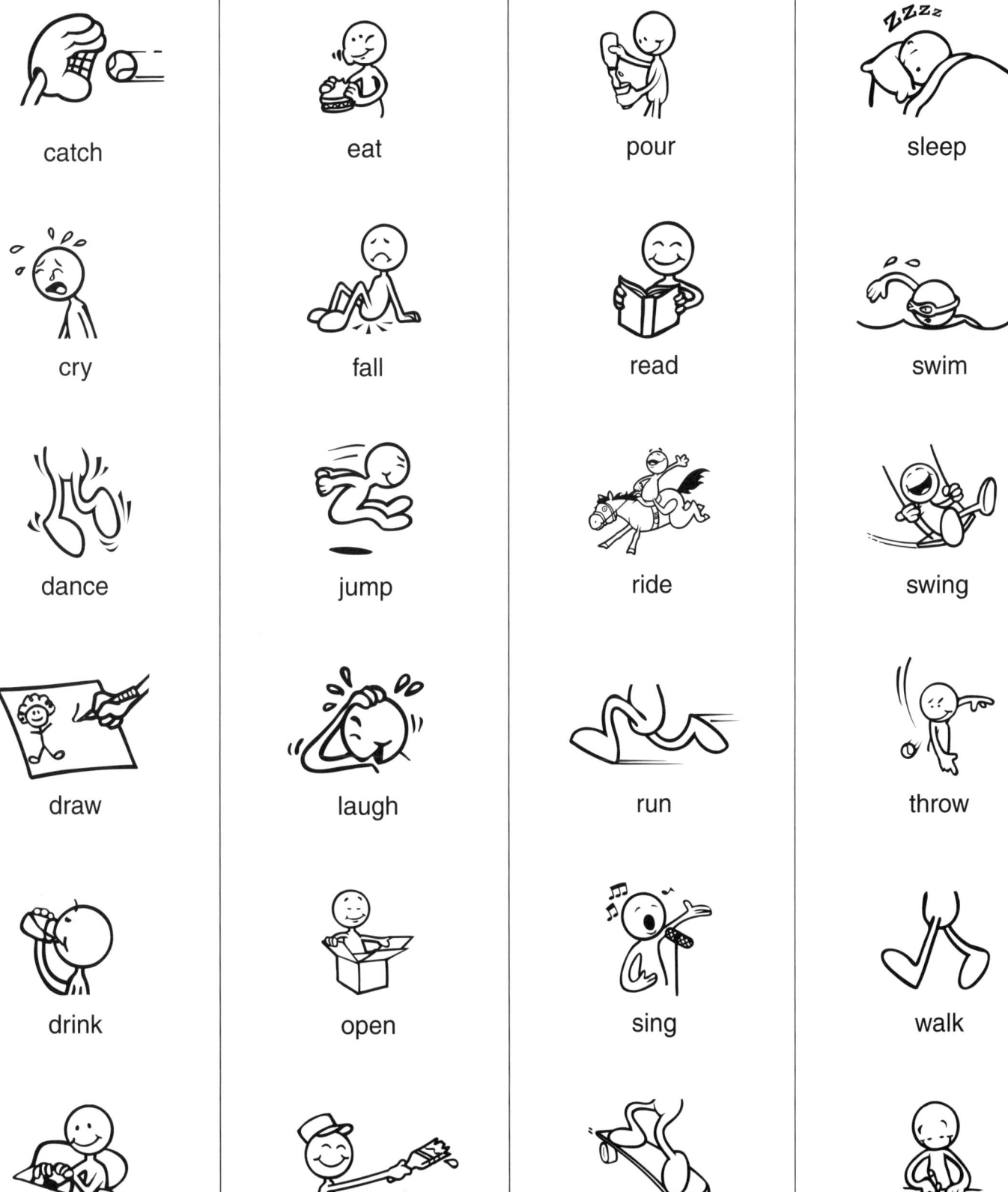

catch	eat	pour	sleep
cry	fall	read	swim
dance	jump	ride	swing
draw	laugh	run	throw
drink	open	sing	walk
drive	paint	skateboard	write

Subject/Verb Agreement Plural

Directions: Use these words to help complete the stories on pages 201 to 205 and 210 to 214.

❏ act	❏ give	❏ smile
❏ bake	❏ help	❏ snow
❏ bark	❏ hide	❏ spend
❏ bathe	❏ hold	❏ spill
❏ bend	❏ hop	❏ splash
❏ blow	❏ hug	❏ study
❏ break	❏ jump	❏ surf
❏ brush	❏ laugh	❏ surprise
❏ build	❏ listen	❏ sweep
❏ call	❏ look	❏ swim
❏ carry	❏ march	❏ swing
❏ catch	❏ meow	❏ taste
❏ chase	❏ open	❏ teach
❏ chew	❏ paint	❏ tear
❏ choose	❏ paste	❏ throw
❏ clap	❏ pitch	❏ tickle
❏ clean	❏ plant	❏ twist
❏ climb	❏ play	❏ walk
❏ close	❏ pour	❏ wash
❏ color	❏ pull	❏ watch
❏ comb	❏ push	❏ wave
❏ cough	❏ rain	❏ work
❏ crawl	❏ reach	❏ wrap
❏ cry	❏ read	❏ write
❏ cut	❏ ride	❏ yawn
❏ dance	❏ ring	❏ yell
❏ draw	❏ roll	❏ zip
❏ dream	❏ row	
❏ dress	❏ run	
❏ drink	❏ sew	
❏ drive	❏ share	
❏ eat	❏ shop	
❏ fall	❏ sing	
❏ feed	❏ skateboard	
❏ fix	❏ ski	
❏ fly	❏ sleep	
❏ fold	❏ slide	

#BK-309 Grammar Tickle Stories™ • ©2004 Super Duper® Publications • 1-800-277-8737 • Online! www.superduperinc.com

The Critics Agree. . . Movie Review

Directions: Give each student a list of the Picture Words on page 199 or the Word List on page 200. Do not reveal the story title. Ask the student for "words" from his/her page to fill in the spaces in the story below. Write the words in the spaces. You may also have the student write these words on his/her Companion Activity Sheet (page 206). Then, have the student read/listen to the story. For more options, see *How To Use This Book* on page ii.

It is the premier of *Widgets In Wonderland*. Here is one reporter's story.

"I am watching the lights _____. The actors _____, and
(subject/verb plural)   (subject/verb plural)

for a moment, moms and dads _____. There are times, when old and
(subject/verb plural)

young alike, laugh, cry and _____. The plot is exciting and filled with fun
(subject/verb plural)

characters, such as the Widgets. Widgets are tiny creatures who _____
(subject/verb plural)

when you least expect it. The Hokies are also creatures who _____,
(subject/verb plural)

many times, during this family movie. Let's interview a grandmother who has taken her

grandchildren to this show. 'In most movies, the characters _____,' she
(subject/verb plural)

said. 'In *Widgets in Wonderland*, they _____.' So, there you have it, folks.
(subject/verb plural)

It's a movie treat for the whole family. Now, back to you, Alice."

Questions: (Answer in a complete sentence.)
- ❏ 1. According to this article, what do the lights do first?
- ❏ 2. According to the article, what do actors do?
- ❏ 3. According to the article, what do the Widgets do?
- ❏ 4. According to the article, what do the Hokies do?
- ❏ 5. According to the grandmother, what do characters in most movies do?

Homework: Take a copy of this story and word/picture list home, and follow the directions above.

_____   _____   _____
Name   Homework Partner   Date

**Subject/Verb
Agreement
Plural**

Costume Shop

Directions: Give each student a list of the Picture Words on page 199 or the Word List on page 200. Do not reveal the story title. Ask the student for "words" from his/her page to fill in the spaces in the story below. Write the words in the spaces. You may also have the student write these words on his/her Companion Activity Sheet (page 206). Then, have the student read/listen to the story. For more options, see *How To Use This Book* on page ii.

Welcome to the *COSTUME SHOP*, your one stop shopping place for funny faces,

crazy costumes, and wild and wooly wigs! First, in the Alien Costume Sections, you'll

see costumes that _____! They practically _____ right off
(subject/verb plural)   (subject/verb plural)

the hangers! Aliens have weird faces that _____, so the masks are
(subject/verb plural)

downright scary! If you think aliens have hair, then our wigs will _____ for
(subject/verb plural)

you! If you think they don't, then our hats might _____ for you! In the
(subject/verb plural)

Wizard of Oz section, you'll see how *The Tin Man* and *The Scarecrow*

_____. If they only had a heart and a brain! *Dorothy's* ruby slippers
(subject/verb plural)

_____ when you click them. Also, don't forget the loveable *Cowardly Lion*.
(subject/verb plural)

Boys and girls _____, just like the Lion, when they put that costume on!
(subject/verb plural)

Our costumes are *GRRRRReat*!!!

Questions: (Answer in a complete sentence.)

- ❏ 1. What do alien costumes practically do right off the hangers?
- ❏ 2. What might the alien wigs do for you?
- ❏ 3. What do *The Tin Man* and *Scarecrow* costumes do?
- ❏ 4. What can *Dorothy's* ruby slippers do?
- ❏ 5. What do boys and girls do like *Cowardly Lion* when they put his costume on?

Homework: Take a copy of this story and word/picture list home, and follow the directions above.

_____   _____   _____   **Subject/Verb Agreement Plural**
Name   Homework Partner   Date

#BK-309 Grammar Tickle Stories™ • ©2004 Super Duper® Publications • 1-800-277-8737 • Online! www.superduperinc.com

Scout's Honor

Directions: Give each student a list of the Picture Words on page 199 or the Word List on page 200. Do not reveal the story title. Ask the student for "words" from his/her page to fill in the spaces in the story below. Write the words in the spaces. You may also have the student write these words on his/her Companion Activity Sheet (page 206). Then, have the student read/listen to the story. For more options, see *How To Use This Book* on page ii.

Today is the first meeting of *Super Scouts*. For those of you who are new to

scouting, I'm going to go over a few of our basic rules. But, before we start, it is most

important that all Scouts _____.
　　　　　　　　　　　　　　(subject/verb plural)

1. Scouts never _____ until they get permission from their Scout Leader.
　　　　　　　　(subject/verb plural)

2. Scouts raise their hand if they need to _____, instead of shouting it out.
　　　　　　　　　　　　　　　　　　　(subject/verb plural)

3. During our field training, we use the buddy system. That means that all Scouts must

_____ with a buddy at all times.
　(subject/verb plural)

4. Scouts are always honest. Scouts _____ if they see someone doing
　　　　　　　　　　　　　　　　　(subject/verb plural)

   something dishonest.

5. Have fun! After all, if Scouts can't _____ and have fun doing it, what's
　　　　　　　　　　　　　　　　　　(subject/verb plural)

   the point of being in scouting?

6. At all times, Scouts must _____. This shows respect for their
　　　　　　　　　　　　　(subject/verb plural)

   Scout Leaders.

Now, Scouts, go out there and _____!
　　　　　　　　　　　　　　(subject/verb plural)

Questions: (Answer in a complete sentence.)
- ❏ 1. Before we start, what must all Scouts do?
- ❏ 2. According to rule #1, what must Scouts never do without permission?
- ❏ 3. What must Scouts do with a buddy during field training?
- ❏ 4. What should Scouts do if they see someone doing something dishonest?
- ❏ 5. What do most Scouts do to show respect?

Homework: Take a copy of this story and word/picture list home, and follow the directions above.

Name	Homework Partner	Date

Subject/Verb Agreement Plural

A Radio Show at the Park

Directions: Give each student a list of the Picture Words on page 199 or the Word List on page 200. Do not reveal the story title. Ask the student for "words" from his/her page to fill in the spaces in the story below. Write the words in the spaces. You may also have the student write these words on his/her Companion Activity Sheet (page 206). Then, have the student read/listen to the story. For more options, see *How To Use This Book* on page ii.

Hello listeners! This is your radio host, Seldom Scene, coming from the grand opening

of the *Park 'n Play Park*. Since you can't "see" me, I'm going to try and give you an idea of

what is going on here today. I can see the happy children _____. They
(subject/verb plural)

throw bread to the ducks, who _____ when they see it. The grown-ups
(subject/verb plural)

_____ when they see how happy the children are. The dogs
(subject/verb plural)

_____ when they see a ball fly by. It's beautiful here. The leaves on the
(subject verb plural)

trees _____ in the wind. The kites _____ on their strings.
(subject/verb plural) (subject/verb plural)

Flowers _____ in colorful bunches. We'll be here until 5 o'clock today. We
(subject/verb plural)

hope you'll come and join the fun. Remember, friends who _____ together
(subject/verb plural)

form long lasting friendships. This is Seldom Scene, reporting live from *Park 'n Play Park*.

Questions: (Answer in a complete sentence.)

❏ 1. What does the radio host say that happy children do?

❏ 2. What does the radio host say ducks do when they see bread?

❏ 3. What does the radio host say the dogs do when a ball is thrown?

❏ 4. What does the radio host say the leaves do in the wind?

❏ 5. What does the radio host say that friends do together?

Homework: Take a copy of this story and word/picture list home, and follow the directions above.

_____ _____ _____
Name Homework Partner Date

Subject/Verb Agreement Plural

#BK-309 *Grammar Tickle Stories*™ • ©2004 Super Duper® Publications • 1-800-277-8737 • Online! www.superduperinc.com

Building Blocks City

Directions: Give each student a list of the Picture Words on page 199 or the Word List on page 200. Do not reveal the story title. Ask the student for "words" from his/her page to fill in the spaces in the story below. Write the words in the spaces. You may also have the student write these words on his/her Companion Activity Sheet (page 206). Then, have the student read/listen to the story. For more options, see *How To Use This Book* on page ii.

Welcome to *Building Blocks City*. I am your tour guide. When people see these

amazing structures, they _____. Your eyes will _____ ! Over
$\qquad$ (subject/verb plural) $\qquad$ (subject/verb plural)

here is *Robodog*, made completely out of tiny blocks. See how his arms

_____. It's so lifelike! Next to him, the *Block Volcanoes*
(subject/verb plural)

_____ . If you step over to the right, you can see the huge *Block Moon*.
(subject/verb plural)

There are even *Block Stars* that _____ when the sun goes down! It takes
(subject/verb plural)

years to become a builder. In this next room, you'll see our students _____
(subject/verb plural)

and the teachers _____ . They are working hard. Last, on our tour, is the
(subject/verb plural)

Block Castle. The King and Queen are so lifelike, that you might think they

_____ !
(subject/verb plural)

Now it's time to board our bus and ... oh, wait, that one is made out of blocks! Say, who

took our bus????

Questions: (Answer in a complete sentence.)
❏ 1. What will your eyes do when you see the amazing structures?
❏ 2. What do *Robodog's* arms do?
❏ 3. What do the *Block Stars* do?
❏ 4. What will you see the students and teachers do in the next room?
❏ 5. What might you think the King and Queen do?

Homework: Take a copy of this story and word/picture list home, and follow the directions above.

_____	_____	_____	**Subject/Verb Agreement Plural**
Name	Homework Partner	Date	

Subject/Verb Agreement Plural Companion Activity Sheet

Directions: During or following the story, have the student write words from the word or picture list on the lines below. Then, have the student write sentences with these words in them.

Example: _____ *laugh* _____

_____ *The children **laugh** at the clown.* _____

1. _____

_____

2. _____

_____

3. _____

_____

4. _____

_____

5. _____

_____

6. _____

_____

7. _____

_____

8. _____

_____

Homework: Take a copy of this sheet home with a word/picture list. Then, follow the directions above.

_____ _____ _____

| Name | Homework Partner | Date |

Subject/Verb Agreement Plural

#BK-309 Grammar Tickle Stories™ • ©2004 Super Duper® Publications • 1-800-277-8737 • Online! www.superduperinc.com

What Goes There - The Sequel??

Directions: Read the following paragraphs and decide what's wrong in each sentence. Fix it by writing (or have someone write for you) the correct form of the verb on the line.

1. Boys and girls **applauds** as the curtain is raised. _____

   The widgets **jumps** out from behind a tree when you least expect it! _____

2. The alien costumes almost **leaps** off the rack! _____

   Dorothy's slippers **glows** bright red when you click the heels together. _____

3. Scouts never **leaves** camp without permission. _____

   Scouts must **hikes** with a buddy at all times. _____

   If Scouts **litters**, you must report it. _____

4. At the park, happy children **plays** on the swings. _____

   The ducks **swims** in the lake. _____

   The kites **blows** in the wind. _____

5. At *Block City*, you won't **believes** your eyes. _____

   The *Block Volcanoes* **explodes**. _____

   The *Block Stars* **twinkles**. _____

   In the block castle, the King and Queen **bows** to you. _____

Homework: ❑ Say each correct verb form in your own sentence.

❑ _____.

_____ _____ _____

Name   Homework Partner   Date

Subject/Verb Agreement Plural

Fill in the sentences with the correct subject/verb agreement form. Answer in a complete sentence.

1. The twins _____ the same and it's hard to tell them apart.

2. When the twins _____ at the same time, it always makes us laugh.

_____
Name

_____
Date

Subject/Verb Agreement Plural

Fill in the sentences with the correct subject/verb agreement form. Answer in a complete sentence.

1. The Widgets in Wonderland love to _____ all day.

2. When the Widgets _____, the audience yells, "MORE!"

_____
Name

_____
Date

Subject/Verb Agreement Plural

Fill in the sentences with the correct subject/verb agreement form. Answer in a complete sentence.

1. The ducks in the park love to _____ around the lake.

2. When the ducks get out of the lake, they _____.

_____
Name

_____
Date

Subject/Verb Agreement Plural

Fill in the sentences with the correct subject/verb agreement form. Answer in a complete sentence.

1. The children in the park love to _____.

2. The children in the park _____ when they see the ducks.

_____
Name

_____
Date

Subject / Verb Agreement Plural

#BK-309 Grammar Tickle Stories™ • ©2004 Super Duper® Publications • 1-800-277-8737 • Online! www.superduperinc.com

Subject/Verb Agreement Plural

Fill in the sentences with the correct subject/verb agreement form. Answer in a complete sentence.

1. The astronauts _____ their spaceship.

2. When the astronauts land on the moon, they _____ .

_____ _____
Name   Date

Subject/Verb Agreement Plural

Fill in the sentences with the correct subject/verb agreement form. Answer in a complete sentence.

1. My sister and I _____ with our toys.

2. We _____ so nicely together that our mom takes us for ice cream.

_____ _____
Name   Date

Subject/Verb Agreement Plural

Fill in the sentences with the correct subject/verb agreement form. Answer in a complete sentence.

1. The cowboys _____ the horses around the corral.

2. The horses _____ for the cowboys.

_____ _____
Name   Date

Subject/Verb Agreement Plural

Fill in the sentences with the correct subject/verb agreement form. Answer in a complete sentence.

1. When Scouts _____ in the woods, they never do it alone.

2. Scouts always _____ in pairs or in groups for safety.

_____ _____
Name   Date

Subject/Verb Agreement Plural

Life on the Farm

Directions: Give each student a list of the Picture Words on pages 188 and 199 or the Word Lists on pages 189 and 200. Do not reveal the story title. Ask the student for "words" from his/her page to fill in the spaces in the story below. Write the words in the spaces. You may also have the student write these words on his/her Companion Activity Sheet (page 215). Then, have the student read/listen to the story. For more options, see *How To Use This Book* on page ii.

Have you ever wondered what living on a farm might be like? The rooster

_____, first thing in the morning, to wake everyone up! When the
(subject/verb singular)

chickens see this, they _____ their eggs immediately! The farmer's wife
(subject/verb plural)

comes in and _____ the eggs. You would think this would upset the
(subject/verb singular)

chickens, but they just _____ happily and lay more eggs. The farmer
(subject/verb plural)

has a very important role. He _____ every day, rain or shine! He
(subject/verb singular)

checks on his cows, who _____ when they see him coming! Then he
(subject/verb plural)

gets on his tractor and _____, while checking on his crops. The
(subject/verb singular)

farmhands _____ when they see him coming. They cheer loudly! So you
(subject/verb plural)

see, the farm is a busy, but happy place to work!

Questions: (Answer in a complete sentence.)

❏ 1. What does the rooster do first thing in the morning?

❏ 2. What do the chickens do when they see the rooster?

❏ 3. What does the farmer's wife do to the eggs?

❏ 4. What do the cows do when they see the farmer coming?

❏ 5. What does the farmer do while checking on his crops?

Homework: Take a copy of this story and word/picture list home, and follow the directions above.

_____   _____   _____

Name   Homework Partner   Date

Subject/Verb Agreement Combo

#BK-309 Grammar Tickle Stories™ • ©2004 Super Duper® Publications • 1-800-277-8737 • Online! www.superduperinc.com

The Shadow Knows

Directions: Give each student a list of the Picture Words on pages 188 and 199 or the Word Lists on pages 189 and 200. Do not reveal the story title. Ask the student for "words" from his/her page to fill in the spaces in the story below. Write the words in the spaces. You may also have the student write these words on his/her Companion Activity Sheet (page 215). Then, have the student read/listen to the story. For more options, see *How To Use This Book* on page ii.

Have you ever watched your shadow? There's a famous poem that goes:

I have a little shadow that _____ *with me.*
(subect/verb singular)
And what can be the use of him is more than I can see.

Your shadow can be a friend. Like friends who _____, your shadow
(subject/verb plural)
_____! Watch your shadow. See how it _____!
(subject/verb singular)   (subject/verb singular)

The rest of the poem goes:

The funniest thing about him is the way he _____.
(subject/verb singular)
Not like when proper children _____, *which is always very slow!*
(subject/verb plural)
And if the sun doesn't come up, shadows don't _____ *at all.*
(subject/verb plural)

The end of the poem says:

Like a lazy little shadow, an errant sleepyhead,

My shadow stayed at home behind me, fast asleep in bed.

Questions: (Answer in a complete sentence.)
- 1. What does the first line of the poem say the shadow does with "me"?
- 2. What do your friends do, and what does your shadow do?
- 3. What do the trees do?
- 4. What do "proper children" do?
- 5. What don't shadows do if the sun doesn't come up?

Homework: Take a copy of this story and word/picture list home, and follow the directions above.

_____   _____   _____
Name   Homework Partner   Date

#BK-309 Grammar Tickle Stories™ • ©2004 Super Duper® Publications • 1-800-277-8737 • Online! www.superduperinc.com

Subject/Verb Agreement Combo

Snow Much Fun

Directions: Give each student a list of the Picture Words on pages 188 and 199 or the Word Lists on pages 189 and 200. Do not reveal the story title. Ask the student for "words" from his/her page to fill in the spaces in the story below. Write the words in the spaces. You may also have the student write these words on his/her Companion Activity Sheet (page 215). Then, have the student read/listen to the story. For more options, see *How To Use This Book* on page ii.

Brandi loves to go into the snow. Brandi and her brothers love to make snowmen

and snow women. First, Brandi takes one scoop of snow and _____ it.
(subject/verb singular)

Then, her brothers take more balls of snow and _____ them. If their snow
(subject/verb plural)

people fall over and _____, they'll prop them back up with a stick! They
(subject/verb plural)

put in coal eyes and a carrot nose and see how they _____. Another fun
(subject/verb plural)

thing to do is sledding. Brandi can sit on a board and it _____ all the way
(subject/verb singular)

down the hill. Other sledders _____ when they see her! She really
(subject/verb plural)

_____! The last thing she likes to do in snow is have a snowball fight with
(subject/verb singular)

her brothers. They always _____ the snowballs, but they miss her! Brandi
(subject/verb plural)

has "snow much" fun every time she plays in the snow that

she never wants to go inside.

Questions: (Answer in a complete sentence.)
- ❑ 1. What does Brandi do with one scoop of snow when making a snowman?
- ❑ 2. What do her brothers do with more balls of snow?
- ❑ 3. What do the coal eyes and carrot nose do?
- ❑ 4. What do sledders do when they see Brandi?
- ❑ 5. What do Brandi's brothers do when they have a snowball fight?

Homework: Take a copy of this story and word/picture list home, and follow the directions above.

_____   _____ _____

Name   Homework Partner   Date

Subject/Verb
Agreement
Combo

A Trip To The Cookie Factory

Directions: Give each student a list of the Picture Words on pages 188 and 199 or the Word Lists on pages 189 and 200. Do not reveal the story title. Ask the student for "words" from his/her page to fill in the spaces in the story below. Write the words in the spaces. You may also have the student write these words on his/her Companion Activity Sheet (page 215). Then, have the student read/listen to the story. For more options, see *How To Use This Book* on page ii.

Welcome to the *Friendly Fudge Cookie Factory*! I'm Frieda Friendly. I'll be your guide.

When we first enter the factory, we see workers _____! They are standing
(subject/verb plural)

by huge machines that _____ the cookies one at a time. This takes a long
(subject/verb plural)

time, but each cookie _____ at its own rate. Every worker
(subject/verb singular)

_____. They show pride in their work. In this next room, we have frosters.
(subject/verb singular)

The frosters _____ every cookie individually. Or, as we like to say, it's just
(subject/verb plural)

icing on the cookie! After the cookie is frosted, it _____ before it goes to the
(subject/verb singular)

wrapping room. There, each wrapper _____ quickly, so that we can get the
(subject/verb singular)

cookies out to the store while they're still warm! The trucks _____ to get
(subject/verb plural)

them there in time. Now to our tasting room where...well, I bet you can guess what we do

there, can't you?

Questions: (Answer in a complete sentence.)
- ❏ 1. What do the workers do when we first enter?
- ❏ 2. What does each cookie do at its own rate?
- ❏ 3. What do the frosters do?
- ❏ 4. What does the cookie need to do before it goes to the wrapping room?
- ❏ 5. What do the trucks do to get the cookies to the store?

Homework: Take a copy of this story and word/picture list home, and follow the directions above.

_____   _____   _____   **Subject/Verb Agreement Combo**
Name   Homework Partner   Date

The Ant and The Grasshopper Years Later

Directions: Give each student a list of the Picture Words on pages 188 and 199 or the Word Lists on pages 189 and 200. Do not reveal the story title. Ask the student for "words" from his/her page to fill in the spaces in the story below. Write the words in the spaces. You may also have the student write these words on his/her Companion Activity Sheet (page 215). Then, have the student read/listen to the story. For more options, see *How To Use This Book* on page ii.

This is Morty Fied reporting...

Do you remember the old story about the ants and the grasshopper? The ants

_____ while the grasshopper _____, until one winter day, the
(subject/verb plural)   (subject/verb singular)

grasshopper runs out of food. He _____, trying to get the ants to help him.
(subject/verb singular)

The ants _____ if the grasshopper promises to store food for the winter.
(subject/verb plural)

Well, it is now years later. We have dropped in to see how they're doing.

Morty: So, how have the winters been lately?

Ants: Good, Morty. The grasshopper _____ all the time now, instead of
(subject/verb singular)

playing his fiddle and dancing.

Grasshopper: Yep, it's true Morty, I'm a new grasshopper because the ants

_____, and that helps keep me in line.
(subject/verb plural)

Ants: The grasshopper _____ better than any insect we know!
(subject/verb singular)

Grasshopper (blushing): Ah, shucks, ants. It makes me feel good to see the ants

_____!
(subject/verb plural)

Well, there you have it folks, another fairy tale ending! Goodbye and good night!

Questions: (Answer in a complete sentence.)
- ❑ 1. What does the reporter (Morty Fied) say the ants do in the "old" story?
- ❑ 2. What does the reporter say the grasshopper does in the "old" story?
- ❑ 3. What do the ants say the grasshopper does now, instead of playing his fiddle?
- ❑ 4. What does the grasshopper say the ants do to help keep him in line?
- ❑ 5. What do the ants do that make the grasshopper feel good?

Homework: Take a copy of this story and word/picture list home, and follow the directions above.

_____ _____ _____
Name   Homework Partner   Date

Subject/Verb Agreement Combo

#BK-309 Grammar Tickle Stories™ • ©2004 Super Duper® Publications • 1-800-277-8737 • Online! www.superduperinc.com

Subject/Verb Agreement Combo Companion Activity Sheet

Directions: During or following the story, have the student write words from the word or picture list on the lines below. Then, have the student write sentences with these words in them.

Example: _____ *dances* _____   - OR -   _____ *draw* _____

*She **dances** to the music on the radio.*   *We **draw** funny cartoons in art class.*

1. _____

_____

2. _____

_____

3. _____

_____

4. _____

_____

5. _____

_____

6. _____

_____

7. _____

_____

8. _____

_____

Homework: Take a copy of this sheet home with a word/picture list. Then, follow the directions above.

_____   _____   _____

Name   Homework Partner   Date

Check Yes or No

Directions: Read the question on the left. Check yes or no in the boxes on the right. Then, say the sentence correctly.

Examples: Is this correct? A dog bark. (No. A dog barks)

Is this correct? Cats meow. (Yes. Cats meow.)

		Yes	No
1. Is this correct?	Grasshoppers jumps.	☐	☐
2. Is this correct?	Ants work hard.	☐	☐
3. Is this correct?	The grasshopper play music.	☐	☐
4. Is this correct?	The rooster crows.	☐	☐
5. Is this correct?	The chicken lays eggs.	☐	☐
6. Is this correct?	The cows moos.	☐	☐
7. Is this correct?	A shadow hide.	☐	☐
8. Is this correct?	Your shadow follow you.	☐	☐
9. Is this correct?	Brandi and her brothers throws snowballs.	☐	☐
10. Is this correct?	A snowman melts in the sun.	☐	☐
11. Is this correct?	A sled slide down a hill.	☐	☐
12. Is this correct?	Bakers bake cookies.	☐	☐
13. Is this correct?	Frosters ices the cookies.	☐	☐
14. Is this correct?	Boys and girls eat the cookies!	☐	☐

Homework: ❑ Say the sentence correctly.

❑ _____.

_____   _____   _____

Name   Homework Partner   Date

Subject/Verb Agreement Combo

#BK-309 Grammar Tickle Stories™ • ©2004 Super Duper® Publications • 1-800-277-8737 • Online! www.superduperinc.com

Subject/Verb Agreement Combo

Fill in the blanks in the sentences with a correct subject/verb agreement form. Then, read the complete sentences.

1. The grasshopper _____ all day while the ants work.

2. The ants _____ all day while the grasshopper plays.

_____ _____
Name   Date

Subject/Verb Agreement Combo

Fill in the blanks in the sentences with a correct subject/verb agreement form. Then, read the complete sentences.

1. The rooster _____ in the morning when the sun rises.

2. The roosters _____ to wake people up on a farm.

_____ _____
Name   Date

Subject/Verb Agreement Combo

Fill in the blanks in the sentences with a correct subject/verb agreement form. Then, read the complete sentences.

1. When winter comes, the ants _____ all the food they saved.

2. The grasshopper _____ nothing, because he played all summer.

_____ _____
Name   Date

Subject/Verb Agreement Combo

Fill in the blanks in the sentences with a correct subject/verb agreement form. Then, read the complete sentences.

1. Chickens _____ eggs in their nest.

2. The farmer collects the eggs that a chicken _____.

_____ _____
Name   Date

Subject / Verb Agreement Combo

Subject/Verb Agreement Combo

Fill in the blanks in the sentences with a correct subject/verb agreement form. Then, read the complete sentences.

1. When you move, your shadow _____ with you.

2. Shadows _____ every time you do.

_____   _____
Name   Date

Subject/Verb Agreement Combo

Fill in the blanks in the sentences with a correct subject/verb agreement form. Then, read the complete sentences.

1. People _____ snowmen out of snow, coal eyes, and a carrot nose.

2. When my dad _____ a snowman, he puts a black top hat on it, like Frosty The Snowman!

_____   _____
Name   Date

Subject/Verb Agreement Combo

Fill in the blanks in the sentences with a correct subject/verb agreement form. Then, read the complete sentences.

1. If you take a snowball, aim and _____ it, it might just plop on the ground!

2. If everyone takes a snowball and _____ it, a snowball fight will start.

_____   _____
Name   Date

Subject/Verb Agreement Combo

Fill in the blanks in the sentences with a correct subject/verb agreement form. Then, read the complete sentences.

1. A cookie must _____ in a warm oven.

2. Cookies _____ in a warm oven to get brown!

_____   _____
Name   Date

Subject / Verb Agreement Combo

#BK-309 Grammar Tickle Stories™ • ©2004 Super Duper® Publications • 1-800-277-8737 • Online! www.superduperinc.com